D1084269

Cutting Up Touches

Cutting Up Touches

A Brief History of Pockets
and the People Who Pick Them

David Avadon

SQUASH PUBLISHING

All photographs are from the author's collection, except: 3 (courtesy of the WG Alma Conjuring Collection, State Library of Victoria, Australia), 36 (courtesy of Christer Nilsson), and 119, 120 and 126 (courtesy of Cicrus Collection Jaap Best, Teylers Museum, Haarlem, The Netherlands).

Book layout and cover design by Gabe Fajuri

Squash Publishing
Chicago, IL 60618
www.squashpublishing.com

ISBN-10: 0-9744681-6-9
ISBN-13: 978-0-9744681-6-7

First Edition
654321

Contents

Profiles in Pickpocketing

Student of Stealth

"Someone has lifted my purse ... he was swifter than any magician." Here is a man who lost his money, yet he cannot help admiring the perpetrator of this crime.

This passage is from the all time best-selling volume on the art of filching, *How to Pick Pockets* by Eddie Joseph (Abbott's Magic Novelty Co., 1940). According to this prolific Bombay baffler, he witnessed the above incident in 1923, and it gave him the idea of weaving pickpocketing stunts into his legerdemain. But what does dipping pockets have to do with the art of simulating wonders? In other words, what's a pickpocket doing in a magic show?

Savvy showmen have always realized that feats which suggest great skill blend well with classical conjuring. Think of Kellar and lightning calculations; Thurston and card scaling; Houdini and escapes; Al Baker and ventriloquism; Slydini and the Paper Balls Over the Head; McGill and hypnosis; Fu Manchu and hand shadows; Jarrow and the eggs and tray inertia feat; Blackstone, Sr.

An ad for Eddie Joseph's classic text, How to Pick Pockets.

and — pickpocketing!

I was drawn to the art of theatrical thievery in my early twenties. Living in Los Angeles, I went to see *It's Magic* in 1973. Featured in the show was Vic Perry, a British pickpocket, hefty in size and stage presence. For twenty minutes spectators weren't entertained; they were riveted. Onlookers weren't laughing; they were roaring.

I came back many times during the run, and night after night Perry garnered huge ovations. In the *Los Angeles Times* review, the reporter gushed when describing Vic's act. Here was a performer who could hold an audience — though hold is too mild a word — for nearly half an hour with no props and no stooges, armed only with skill, humor and daring showmanship. I was smitten. I thought this was the *ne plus ultra* in stagecraft. (Actually, Perry did use one small prop: a little leather bucket. He told the patrons he was going to find coins in their clothing, but none was actually produced as he went through the

Vic Perry, formidable in size and showmanship.

David Avadon ◈ 3

audience searching pockets. The bucket was tossed aside once his caper in the aisles was complete.)

All right, I'm smitten, but where does one go to learn to be a thief? I did have one idea. Growing up in Los Angeles, I'd heard about the great pickpocket Dr. Giovanni from nearly the first moment I declared myself a magician. Whenever I opened my bag of tricks, Giovanni's name seemed to come flying out. People couldn't wait to tell me their stories. Giovanni did tricks on the golf course, at the barber shop, in restaurants, at the Friar's Club (an exclusive show-business institution). And I'd seen reviews of his act in magicians' trade magazines. Would he take on a student? I could ask. I searched out his number, timidly called and explained my hope. He accepted the fee I proposed for lessons, and for the next three months we met twice a week at his apartment in Beverly Hills. Giovanni was then semiretired and in his late seventies. He shared with me his wiles and ruses, his sleights and stratagems, and that was my beginning in this underground art.

The Dip and the Cousin

Of course, the earliest relationship between conjuring and pocket picking was not theatrical but nefarious. The Hieronymus Bosch painting *The Juggler* (c. 1475) tells the story perfectly. The *wiz mob* (pickpocket team) consists of the magician, the child and the *dip artist*. Setting himself up in a fairground or marketplace, the itinerant juggler builds a *tip*, distracting the *mark* with his tricks and giving the *cannon* (pickpocket) a logical reason to stand near the *cousin* (victim). The child is the *stall*, making physical contact with the *mark*, intensifying the distraction. You'll notice the child is not watching the show but the victim, making sure she (yes, *she,* according to Kurt Volkmann in his book *The Oldest Deception*, Carl W. Jones, 1956.) is oblivious to everything but the wizard. The *hook* (the pickpocket) makes the *touch* (lifts her purse), and the

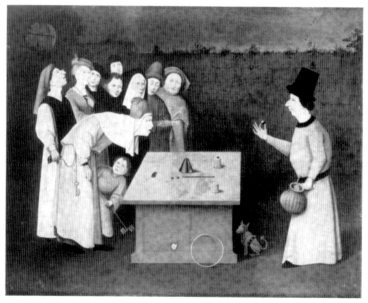

The Juggler *by Hieronymus Bosch ca. 1475.*

team will meet later to *cut up touches* (divvy up the takings). There are, of course, other ways of interpreting this painting (see the Volkmann work), but I wanted to introduce you to the classic members of a *wire mob* (pickpocket team), a cast that hasn't changed in all the 500 years since *The Juggler* was painted. Missing in the Bosch illustration is the *duke man*, the person to whom the *poke* is secretly handed off. The *duke man* is there so the *tool* (pickpocket) will be clean if *the bates tumbles and beefs gun* (if the victim realizes what's happened and calls for a copper). (Note: In the July 2006 issue of *Genii*, Pekka Gunst reveals a joke hidden in *The Juggler* 500 years ago by Hieronymus Bosch. Turn the painting 90 degrees counter clockwise. The table and props become a face, wide eyed with amazement.)

Many aspiring stage pickpockets deepen their knowledge of the art by studying their criminal brethren. If you, too, would like to learn the ways of these sleight-of-pocket grifters, I would direct you first to David W. Maurer's examination of professional pickpockets, *Whiz Mob* (College and University Press, 1964). If Dickens' England is your beat, then look for pickpocketing references in Henry Mayhew's *London Labour and the London Poor*. The career of Jenny Diver, a sobriquet awarded by her fellow *hooks* in recognition of her masterful ability to *dive* into pockets undetected, is outlined in *The Art of Crime* (Philip Allan, 1931). A riveting read is Timothy Gilfoyle's *A Pickpocket's Tale* (W.W. Norton & Company, 2006), a revealing portrait of pickpockets and con-artists in nineteenth-century New York.

A sampling of titles rich in pickpocketing lore includes *Professional Criminals of America* (Cassell & Company, 1886); *Keys to Crookdom* (D. Appleton and Company, 1924); *The Professional Thief* (The University of Chicago Press, 1937); *Dictionary of American Underworld Lingo* (Twayne Publishers, 1950); *The Encyclopedia of American Crime* (Facts on File, 1982) and *Sting Shift*

(Street Smart Communications, 1989).

One synonym for a pickpocket has a fascinating etymology. How did a pickpocket come to be called a *cannon*?

Many early 20th century pickpockets were Jewish. They were called *gonifs*, Yiddish for thief. To non-Yiddish speaking grifters, *gonif* sounded like *gun*. So pickpockets became known as *guns*; their teams were called *gun mobs*. As in the magic world, pickpockets are capable of escalating hyperbole. One pickpocket decided that if the other guy was a *gun,* then he was a *cannon*, and soon *cannon* became the accepted term for all superior *dips*.

In pickpocketing tradition there is one urban legend as confirmed in our imaginations as the tale of Houdini untying knots with his toes. Have you heard of a student pickpocket confronting a coat with bells attached to each pocket, then forced to practice until he can empty the pockets without inciting a single chime? Of course you have. It's everywhere in pickpocketing legend, repeated as fact even in police manuals. But, like the tale of Houdini's talented toes, it just ain't so. The idea may have originated with Charles Dickens when he was imagining Fagin's school for pickpockets in *Oliver Twist*. From there it was picked up by Mayhew, who mistook invention for gospel and inserted the yarn in *London Labour and the London Poor*.

The image of the bell-protected coat may even predate Dickens. In *Complete Course in Pick Pocketing* (Tannen's Magic Manuscript, Ltd., 1983), Pierre Jacques recalls a medieval French folk tale about a man who must steal a bag of gold from a coat pocket without ringing any of the bells which safeguard the pockets. It's quite possible Dickens was familiar with this story and drew on the detail of the bells as the ultimate test of pickpocketing skill. And because it's such an evocative image, the story became permanently associated in our collective fancy with the training of light-fingered swipesmen. But writers aren't pickpockets; neither are cops nor conjurers. A *class cannon* — either stage or street — could tell you that making the *touch* is sometimes deft but just as often rough and always forceful enough to rattle any wind chimes in the path of an exiting wallet. It's effective misdirection and perfect timing which make it possible to *beat the mark for his leather*.

The Myth of the Cannon

To create a buzz, as we say today, itinerant tricksters arriving in town took to self-publishing colorful biographies with tall tales of travel, triumphant command performances, witty practical jokes and hilarious impromptu whimsies. These Scheherazade-like fables became the earliest press releases. The ability to steal from pockets undetected was prominent in many of these imagined accomplishments. Pickpocketing prowess, as Eddie Joseph discovered, ignites the imagination of those in more pedestrian professions.

A favorite tale told by Tobias Bamberg (1812 — 1870) appears in H.J. Burlingame's *Leaves from Conjurers' Scrap Books* (Donohue, Henneberry & Co., 1891, reprinted 2005 by *Magico Magazine*). It seems that Old Bamberg, as he was nicknamed by Dutch fans, was traveling by train from Rotterdam to The Hague via

Delft. He shared a compartment with three other men. As they rattled along, he asked one fellow the time, and the chap discovered his watch missing; the second passenger checked his own pockets and found his handkerchief absent; the last man hurriedly fingered his uniform and was astonished to find his purse had vanished. Suspicion fell on Bamberg. When the train reached The Hague, the three victims complained to the Commissionaire of Police, and the group was taken to the office of the Inspector of Police. After the trio told their tale of loss, Old Bamberg calmly told them to look at the boot of the third victim, a dragoon. The chain of the missing timepiece could be seen hanging therefrom, and a quick search revealed all the missing articles therein. The Inspector of Police began to recognize Old Bamberg, the best known bamboozler (a word which possibly comes from the name Bamberg) in Holland, who then revealed his identity and received compliments from all on his masterly pickpocketing prank.

In *Herrmann the Great* (Laird & Lee, 1897), another book by Burlingame, he bubbles with excitement when describing the pickpocketing skills of the brothers Herrmann — Compars, who began his performing career in the 1840s, and Alexander, who took to the stage a decade later. Compars, he avers, could arrive at a crowded gathering and, within five minutes, reach into a hat and produce items stolen from every person in the room, each returned with an appropriate bon mot. In another publicity puff, Compars is portrayed as the victim. It seems he went to view a Patagonian village brought to Paris as an exhibition. He was accompanied by several notables who found it charming to see Herrmann astonish these wild natives with his wonderments. After leaving the exhibit, one of his companions asked the time, and Compars discovered that, while he had been amusing the savages with tricks, a Patagonian dip had purloined his watch!

Burlingame repeats one of Alexander Herrmann's favorite tales of picking pockets for notoriety. While appearing at the Egyptian Hall in England, he conceived a stunt to garner press coverage. On a crowded street, he allowed two London bobbies to "accidentally" observe him emptying a pocket. When they accused him of the theft, he insisted on being searched. The shakedown revealed neither of two missing items. Then Alexander insisted the policemen search themselves. In the pocket of one, a stolen handkerchief was discovered, and, in the pocket of the other, the victim's watch, much to the embarrassment of the gendarmes and the squealing delight of the assembled passersby. Other versions of this story have even more elaborate revelations of stolen items when the officers dutifully drag Herrmann to the station house. These are appealing legends, repeated by enraptured reporters and unquestioned by generations of magi. (Obvious to all is the suspicious similarity between the Bamberg and Herrmann confections)

Did they happen? It's likely they were inventions meant to pique the interest of theater patrons, although there is a passage in *Leaves from Conjurers' Scrap Books* which suggests there may have been some pickpocketing in Alexander's stage show. The author describes amateur magicians preparing to go to Herrmann's performance by loading their pockets "with packs of cards, for the sake of having him [Herrmann] pull them out in the presence of the audience...." On the other hand, in *The Old & the New Magic* (The Open Court Publishing Company, 1909), Henry Ridgely Evans describes a day spent with Alexander as he walked the streets of Baltimore publicizing his show with fabulous impromptu feats. In Evans' description, there is no mention of even the tiniest theft during an entire afternoon of conjuring, suggesting pocket picking was not de rigueur in Alexander's promotional sorcery.

Pickpockets Stumble into the Spotlight

Jasper Maskelyne was one of many tricksters inspired to pilfer a pocket for entertainment purposes. In recounting his memories of Jasper, Clive Court described coming forward as a volunteer to help the famous wizard with a coffin escape. At the end of his stint on stage, the amateur was chagrined to learn that Maskelyne had picked his pocket. And what did Maskelyne nick from this budding mystifier? A wallet fat with bills? A gold cigarette case? No. A Ball and Vase which Jasper proceeded to perform to the great amusement of the audience. It was a whimsical touch of burglary never forgotten by Court.

If Maskelyne was one of many magicians to combine poaching with presto, then who was the first to build an act entirely around on-stage stealing? According to Topper Martyn: Fred Brezin. Says Martyn (*Genii*, July 1993),

"Fred Brezin was perhaps the first comedy pickpocket magician. Brezin was born in France in 1886 and by 1900 was working in the London Theatres [*sic*] as Master Fred, The Boy Magician. In 1906 he was featuring pickpocket business in his comedy magic act." A reference in *British Music Hall* by Roy Busby (Paul Elek Limited, 1976) says he introduced his deft pickpocket routine while on the bill of the Canterbury Music Hall. Harry Stanley, in *Magic on the Halls* (Unique Magic, n.d.), places the debut a couple of years later and says the spot was titled "Fred Brezin, The Light-Fingered Magician."

Before I introduce the performers who are about to emerge as sensations in this new specialty, I'd like to explain the five ways a performer can create the illusion of pickpocketing ability: (1) *Genuine skill.* The pickpocket may case the audience looking for spectators wearing or carrying the things he likes to steal (just as a street pickpocket would), but the lifting is real; the performer is at risk every moment. (2) *Instant stooge.* While a show is in progress, the performer or an assistant cues one or more volunteers to play along with the faux pickpocketing. (3) *Stooges.* One or more audience members are brought backstage before a show and asked to help the pickpocket in any of several different ways. (4) *Horses (*also called *barons).* A pickpocket may use paid assistants who travel with the performer and pretend to be spectators from the audience. (5) *Inference.* This is the suggestion that pickpocketing has occurred. There are many ways a performer can infer pickpocketing.

Here's one example: The pickpocket briefly handles a spectator, then returns his wallet, watch, comb and pen. The spectator is genuinely amazed. The watch and wallet have actually been swiped, and it's their appearance the fellow is reacting to. The comb and pen (inexpensive items provided by the showman) are flashed to the audience, then quickly tucked into the fellow's pockets. The inference is that four items have been smartly stolen instead of two. As you will see ahead, the enterprising *hook* may combine more than one technique in crafting his turn.

In the 1920s the idea of the pickpocket specialist began to percolate in the imaginations of sleight-of-hand artists. Jean Arnolis from Belgium experimented with several different acts, one of which was a pickpocket spot performed in 1926 under the name Jean Lupin. In 1928 *Doublings, der Manipulator als Pickpocket* appeared in Germany (self-published by the author, Walter Breucker, under his nom de plume Brewalt Ucker). It's the first book written for magicians that encourages stealing from a spectator and teaches techniques for so doing.

During that same year, Walter Sealtiel (1890 — 1948) became the earliest performer to wow New York audiences with pickpocketing stunts. The uniqueness of his turn brought him plum bookings on the Keith circuit. This "King of Pickpockets" (the first of several entertainers to so crown himself) appeared before many nabobs of the era, including the Prince of Wales, the Prince of Monaco, William Randolph Hearst and

Franklin Delano Roosevelt. Magicians particularly appreciated his clever opening featuring the multiple color-changing necktie. (The method was possibly that of Sam Dreillinger.) Sealtiel, Jewish and born in Berlin, was living in Amsterdam in 1940. He was sent to a Nazi work camp when the Germans invaded Holland. Sealtiel survived the war, but not by much. He returned to Amsterdam where he died in 1948.

Giovanni

Earlier I mentioned Eddie Joseph's teaching text, *How to Pick Pockets*. Canny magicians believe the book was written as a direct response to the roaring success of just one sensational wallet snaffler, the same wallet snaffler who claimed he was kidnapped by Russian circus performers at age two and a half and forced to become an acrobat, who claimed to be a medical doctor, who claimed to have cured fifteen cases of shell shock in World War I with hypnotism, who claimed to have stolen Franklin Delano Roosevelt's watch four times, who claimed to have stolen Winston Churchill's suspenders and returned them, who claimed to be wearing J. Edgar Hoover's suspenders because he stole them and never gave them back. Who is this snaffler of all snafflers? Dr. John Giovanni, The Amazing Giovanni, and sometimes just Giovanni. While claims are not always testifiable truth, one fact is unwavering: In the 1930s and '40s, Dr. Giovanni was, as one magazine writer dubbed him, "The

Dr. Giovanni flashes thirty-dollar watch and million dollar smile.

Deftest Pickpocket in the World."

Though he adopted an Italian *nom de magique*, he was born in Budapest as Adolf Herczog in 1896. He began entertaining in European music halls with a routine of card tricks performed for a committee brought onto the stage. One night he nipped a helper's handkerchief during a show, and the response to this mischief was so great, he began devising other pickpocketing feats. By the mid-1920s he was performing at the Cafe de Paris in London, his basic repertoire already established: a transposition of borrowed bills in spectators' hands, the Ring on Stick and a dramatic version of Comte's "The Ladies' Looking-Glass." The tricks connected his pickpocketing forays. To simply list his tricks, as Harry Stanley says, "... does him an injustice, for not only was he a fine conjuror, he also had charm, personality, and was a great performer. In my talks to magical societies, I dwell at length on the different aspects of his work — real lessons in the presentation of magic."

Giovanni's great publicity coup came at an exclusive London nightclub. He managed to lift something — a stickpin, it is said — from H.R.H. Edward, Prince of Wales, heir to the British throne. The next day the papers were full of the story. The Amazing Giovanni's fees soared as did the demand for his theatrical services. Dai Vernon was the first to tell me this story, and I've since read it elsewhere. But though he chats at length about his chummy relations with many British royals, Giovanni doesn't mention this episode at all in an extensive interview given after his arrival in America several years later.

I was fascinated to discover that when Giovanni first garnered press with his exhibition burglary, some magicians were put off by the rubric *Pickpocket*, considering it crude, unsavory. In the January 1930 issue of the *Linking Ring*, H. Sara, the British correspondent scowled, "To describe himself as a pickpocket may be in very bad taste but from the point of view of publicity it apparently goes quite well...."

By 1933 Giovanni was in the States fracturing audiences with his fractured English. Not his mastery of the language, but his ability to be barely understood was a great part of his charm (and a potent tool for misdirection) on stage. Giovanni spoke — or at least was misunderstood — in many languages, languages which became his passport to travel the world with his taking ways. Other European pickpockets who followed were also polyglots, which made it possible for them, like Giovanni, to export their talents.

He became known by his catch phrase, "No funny business." It meant — well, I don't know what it meant, which is probably why it was such a great slogan. But the Colgate-Palmolive company seemed to know exactly what he was saying. They decided to put out a promotional deck of cards touting the magic powers of their new brushless shaving cream. At the height of his fame, Dr. Giovanni was one of the most recognizable wonder workers in America. He was chosen as the face of

*Dr. Giovanni promises
"No Funny Business" — whatever
that means.*

magic for these cards. His smiling image and nonsensical motto adorned every card Colgate printed.

"No funny business" might have meant "Don't mess with me, or I'll yank your underpants off," or he might have been saying "I don't use any stooges." The latter was certainly true. Early in his career he experimented with the stunts made possible by confederates, but he wisely decided to leave the staged sight gags to others and concentrate on really fooling his helpers. He had another apothegm he hurled at the committee during his act: "If you feel me, you tell me." In other words, "If you catch me picking your pocket, you're free to tell the audience." Daring! But that was Giovanni. He was unquestionably one of the most successful, sought after, highly paid magicians of the nightclub era.

Like Alexander Herrmann, Giovanni was Giovanni wherever he went, ready to launch into a miracle or six whenever he was recognized. One magician arrived early to see Giovanni's nightclub act and found him regaling the busboys with his tricks. He often performed in Las Vegas when Las Vegas was inventing itself and on television variety shows when they, too, were inventing themselves. He died in 1977.

Dr. Giovanni's imprint on conjuring and conjurors is greater than one might imagine. References to his hugely popular turn can be found in *Programs of Famous Magicians* (Magic Incorporated, 1974), *Spotlight on 101 Great Magic Acts* (Micky Hades, 1975) and throughout the run of the *Jinx*. He's profiled in magic histories penned by James Randi (*Conjuring*, St. Martin's Press, 1992) and John Booth (*Dramatic Magic*, Ridgeway Press, 1988). He was one of the architects of this specialty act and its most recognizable exponent in America for more than thirty years. Intense curiosity about his techniques provoked the publication of Eddie Joseph's teaching

Okito (Theo. Bamberg, left) and Dr. Giovanni. Both Jewish and both great artists in very different ways.

tome (mentioned earlier), which is still purchased by thousands every year. Al Koran became enamored with the Ring on Stick as performed by Dr. Giovanni. Although he modified the handling to suit his taste, the structure of Koran's routine duplicates Giovanni's exactly. Giovanni's repertoire of pocket tricks included several versions of Free and Unlimited Coinage of Silver, all of which featured coins appearing under salt shakers. "Say, you don't mean — ?" Yes, seeing Giovanni ignited the imagination of Al Goshman for whom finding coins under salt shakers became the basis of one of the most beautiful table-top performances ever conceived. And finally, there's Tihany. As a young magician in Hungary, Tihany was so entranced with Giovanni that he peeked into a music hall (a place where children were verboten) night after night just to see this master showman. Thrilled by Giovanni, he created a pickpocketing routine for his own show. It became a comic highlight for years.

Borra

If Giovanni was the face of fleecing in America, then surely Boris Borra was the godfather of grabbing, the patron picker of purses, in Europe. He happened to be in Jagodina, Serbia when he was born Borislav Milojkowic in 1921, but that was just the first stop in his tours around the world. There's Borra now, entering the Bertram Mills Circus riding an elephant, billed as "The Thief of Bagdad." He stuns the audience by immediately

Borra, King of Pickpockets and pickpocket of kings.

returning stolen items, items lifted from patrons seated throughout the audience. But how? Borra never came near them. (They've forgotten the bumbling usher who showed them to their seats.) His feats are daring. He seems to steal a watch while a spectator's hand is tightly clamped over the timepiece. He steals a pair of glasses, not from a volunteer's pocket, but from his very face. His finale involves lifting a necktie from one spectator and a pair of suspenders from another and squeezing every drop of comedy out of the situation before their eventual return.

On nightclub stages Borra appeared in a tailcoat with a cape and top hat. He produced cigarettes and billiard balls and essayed ever so delicate stunts with smoke rings. Borra sometimes partnered with his wife, Ilse, for a duet of dipping. Borra would stand in front of a volunteer, his wife behind. As Borra adroitly emptied the person's pockets, he passed each item behind the victim to Ilse, who held the articles in the air for the audience to see. It was balletic thievery and greatly magnified the theatrical impact of his performance.

Borra became one of the highest earning variety acts in Europe, a favorite of Princess Grace and the royal family of Monaco, and demand for his services was so great that there was simply no room for retirement in his datebook. But before any of this could happen, he had to make it through World War II, a horror which two of his brothers did not survive. In 1947, Arnold Gingrich, one of the most honored editors at *Esquire* Magazine, came to Vienna in search of stories about post-war Europe. An accidental discovery caught his imagination — Borra! At the time, Borra appeared in two Vienna nightclubs and was the most sought-after entertainer for every prestigious military dinner. Gingrich was agog at Borra's talents and became panegyrist for the pickpocketeer and chronicler of a city which had become more ash heap than metropolis. His article appeared in the January 1948 issue of *Esquire* and conjures up images of Carol Reed's great film *The Third Man*. It is the most powerful endorsement of any entertainer I have ever read and the most heart-wrenching depiction of Displaced Persons in war-crushed Europe.

With Borra's multilingual abilities, he was able to appear in half a dozen European circuses and in nightclubs around the world. English was one of his acquisitions, though as Gingrich put it, "Borra...uses the English language with the confident inaccuracy of a drunk at the controls of a jet bomber." He died of a heart attack in 1998. Borra never used stooges. For over half a century, beneath thousands of spotlights, he faced audiences with only his formidable skill and persuasive showmanship. For detailed depictions of Borra's show business odyssey, read *Borra, King of Pickpockets* by John Fisher (*Genii*, March 1996) and *A Conversation with Borra*, David Avadon (*MAGIC,* January 1997 — see page 115). His son, Charlie Borra, continues the family klepto business in European circuses.

Borra's techniques and routines so completely defined

the art of theatrical fleecing in Europe that he became an unintentional Fagin. Numbers of Artful Dodgers sprang up hoping to rival Borra's accomplishments, and many began their careers in dipping by pinching Borra's moves and bits of business.

One Scandinavian performer strongly influenced by Borra was Danish-born Tommy Willy Jörgen Iversen, whose suave pseudonym was Gentleman Jack. Gentleman Jack Atkins (1921 — 1984) could mulct spectators in eight different languages and traveled to twenty different countries (some accounts say more), garnering publicity wherever he went. He appeared in many of the grand circuses of Europe. And when his wife, May, stood behind Jack's volunteers to act as the receiver of stolen goods, that was pure Borra. Copenhagener Kenny Quinn was a student of Gentleman Jack's and is currently a most successful theatrical dip. Svedino (Lennart Svedfelt, 1924 — 1993) worked in public relations for the Swedish Furuvik Circus in 1949, the year Borra was featured as a guest artist. Watching Borra night after night aroused pickpocketing aspirations in the PR man who began practicing Borra's extraction techniques. Five years later Svedino was starring in Circus Zoo while Borra headlined Circus Scott, both Swedish circuses. How delighted was Borra to see his methods and wrinkles aped by the rival performer? Not very.

Perhaps because I'm persuaded by the prolific storyteller Garrison Keillor that Scandinavians are silent and severe, it amazes me that a disproportionately

Gentleman Jack and his genteel abstractions.

Kenny Quinn executes one of Borra's signature steals.

David Avadon ◈ 31

large number of Swedes and Danes are smooth-talking, octopus-fingered pickpockets. Maybe they just want to keep their hands warm in the wintertime! Look for more Scandinavians profiled ahead.

One contemporary, non-Nordic cannon whose techniques for vacuuming pockets largely mimic Borra's is James Freedman from Britain. His clever, self-proclaimed title: James Freedman, "The Man of Steal."

In the late 1940s and early 50s, Zorran became the most brazen of all the Borra imitators. His theatrical name, with its double "r"s was chosen to sound as much like Borra's as possible. He called himself "The Gentleman Pickpocket," a tag influenced, I'm sure, by Gentleman Jack. Zorran shanghaied Borra's entire act, including the smoke rings, and brought it to America. His explanation for this highway — make that low way — robbery? He claimed to be a relative. Was Borra aware of Zorran? Yes. Related to him? No. According to Ricki Dunn, Zorran died a tragic though heroic death. He was shot trying to rescue a woman who was being molested.

World War II Era Pickpocketeers

By the arrival of World War II, the pickpocket act was a clearly defined specialty number. A light-fingered magus of the era was Fred Roner (Alfred Rosner), who left Austria and the Nazis behind in 1939 and emigrated to the United States where he worked professionally as a stage pickpocket.

In England, Sirdani (Sid Daniels, 1900 — 1982) was a familiar figure to doormen in posh London hotels with his red fez and bag of tricks. (This well-known British trickster with a long career might have reconsidered his exotic stage name if he'd known that, to a Sikh, Sirdani is the word for Mrs.) He was a popular performer of pickpocketing stunts in variety theatres and at many fancy dinners. As a soldier in World War I, he amused mates in the trenches with his tricks. When shells exploded in the middle of an experiment, he would exclaim, "Don't be

With his red fez and bag of tricks, Sirdani
brought laughter to music halls and
banquet rooms for generations.

fright!" It became his famous shibboleth. During World War II, he went on the radio and taught a new generation of Tommies simple tricks they could use to entertain during quiet moments. After the war, these broadcasts were collected and published with the title *Don't be Fright: Radio Magic by Sirdani* (Frederick Muller Ltd., 1946).

Rodolfo (Rezsö Gács) was born in Budapest and joined the underground when the Nazis invaded. After the war, he created seventeen different magical routines, one of which featured pickpocketing. He was honored as a performer and teacher of magic in Hungary. The poster proclaiming him a pickpocket can be seen in *100 Years of Magic Posters* (Grosset & Dunlap, 1976).

Dominique

In the 1950s a new kind of pickpocket debuted — Dominique. He was a sensational attraction featured 'round the globe in the largest nightclubs. Opening for stars like Frank Sinatra and Sammy Davis, Jr., Dominique played Ciro's and the Moulin Rouge in Los Angeles as well as the Latin Quarter and Copacabana in New York. If Giovanni was an artistic minimalist, traveling the world with a deck of cards and a couple of gimmicks, Dominique was the performer who combined skillful pickpocketing with showroom spectacle. And French-born Dominique (Dominique Risbourg, c.1932 —) had a theme song! In the early 1960s, the Singing

Dominique reimagined the pickpocket act as artful, hilarious nightclub entertainment.

Nun had recorded *Dominique*. It became a novelty hit heard around the world. Forever after, Dominique was played on with that tune, and audiences were humming his name even before he appeared.

When he did take the stage, it was dimly lit and Dominique, slender and suave, was playing classical guitar. Soon eerie extra hands came crawling around the instrument. Fireflies emerged from the sound hole and whooshed over the heads of the audience, winging all the way to the back of the theater. They returned to Dominique, who held them briefly in his hand. When the fireflies were released, they circled above him, then flew toward a rose attached to the guitar's peg head. Their peregrinations complete, they disappeared into the flower just as the *Malagueña* ended and the spotlight faded to black. Beautiful.

Next, like an enthusiastic host, Dominique worked the ringside tables, greeting patrons, inviting fellows to stand and shake hands. When he returned to the stage, he had an armload of stolen goods, including a woman's purse. An obliging assistant returned the plunder. Next he invited a spectator to join him on stage. Before the gentleman's borrowed bill finally appeared in a cigarette, much pocket picking ensued, including repeat steals of the fellow's watch and a funny gag with his glasses.

Then Dominique threw the stage open to anyone who wanted to join him. Those who came forward were offered seats but hardly got to use them as they became part of the Frenchman's hilarious routine for the Hot Seats (also called the Electric Chairs). As David Devant suggested when he first described this sequence in *Our Magic* (E.P. Dutton and Company; George Routledge and Sons, Ltd., 1911; reprinted by the Fleming Book Company, 1946), magicians need to consider the taste of their audience before deciding to include this piece of business. For nightclub revelers indulging in risqué entertainment, it's perfect. There's something about seeing a man bolt out of a chair as if stung in the rear end by a nuclear-powered wasp that is just — well — funny.

In Dominique's routine, a volunteer is asked to sit in a chair placed on the stage, and almost immediately he jumps up and grabs his rear end. Dominique coaxes the reluctant volunteer to sit down again, promising that nothing will happen, only to have him pop up again the moment his bottom touches the seat. The routine builds gag upon gag until the audience is convulsed with laughter. To cap the routine, all of his volunteers (eight of them) are seated in chairs. Dominique goes down into the audience and asks a man to change chairs with the woman sitting next to him. He says that when he counts three, the man will jump out of his seat. When three is reached, the audience member doesn't flinch — but every one of his volunteers spring from their seats!

Finally, Dominique asks the assistants to stand shoulder to shoulder facing the audience. (The music is racing now.) As Dominique distracts the volunteers, he goes down the row stealing their ties assembly-line fashion. Then he reaches into their coats and snatches off their shirts — even their undershirts. (I expected him to work the line again ripping the tattoos right off their arms!) The assistants race off stage while Dominique bows and the audience roars approval. This was well-choreographed, razzling entertainment. (Dominique's presentations changed as he experimented with new bits of business. Described is the staging of the late 1970s.) Showroom bookers loved it, and in the '60s and '70s Dominique played major Las Vegas casinos and nightclubs around the world, staying for months at a time.

Dominique didn't invent the Hot Seats or the Shirt Pull; magicians had used these pieces of business long before Dominique fashioned his turn. But the tremendous reaction they brought in his act caused pickpockets aplenty to pinch these stunts. They have now become ubiquitous, seen in the acts of theatrical thieves everywhere.

With Dominique it was so long one-man show, hello "It Takes a Village"! A carefully plotted military operation was carried out for every performance (some 38,000 performances, Dominique reckons). Reconnaissance: While the audience awaits the start of the review, his assistant, dressed as a host, visits the tables near the stage, chatting up the guests, making notes on his cuff. (Though it was a gentleman when I saw the show, Dominique told me he most often employed a woman as his helper.) Who has the things Dominique likes to steal? Who would make the best assistant for the

Bill in Cigarette? Which fellows will shine as stooges? Recruitment: Invite eight fellows backstage to teach them their part in the Hot Seats. Prepare their clothing for the Shirt Pull and T-shirt Pull to come. Aide-De-Camp: His assistant is secretly used in the guitar fantasy which opens the show and then appears on stage during the act preparing the volunteers for the tie steal. Weapons array: Genuine pickpocketing, the suggestion of pickpocketing, and stooges — instant and rehearsed — are all elements in this polished entertainment blitz.

Ricki Dunn

Before turning to crime — theatrically speaking — Dominique twice won prizes for Presentation at FISM and charmed elegant nightclub audiences as a ventriloquist. While Dominique moved in these elevated realms, in America another soon-to-be thief was trouping in carnivals as a juggler, fire eater, magician and recliner on a self-constructed bed on nails. This New Jersey-born daredevil, who once escaped from a straightjacket while being dragged around a track by a zooming race car, was befriended by Bruce Elliott and his back room gang. They suggested that the ambitious trickster in search of an act become — *Hmmm, what would be right for this stocky, fiery kid?* Lou Tannen said, "How about becoming — a pickpocket?" And so, with the help of Dr. Jaks and the other denizens of Elliott's New York cabal, Freddy Revello emerged from the back room as Ricki Dunn, "America's

Ricki Dunn — fast, furious and funny!

Funniest Pickpocket."

Silver-haired Ricki Dunn (1929 — 1999) created a powerhouse act perfect for the 1950s night life in which he flourished. He took the European pickpocket act, married it with brash nightclub humor and created one of the classic turns in American variety entertainment. He achieved early success when he was invited to play the Palace at a time when few magicians could get past the stage door. He was solidly booked in the best Miami hotels of the 1950s, a date-getter without equal in Chicago, a show-stopper in the Vegas showrooms of the 1960s, and a cruiseship stellar favorite for many seasons.

Without the multilingual skills of continental pickpockets, Ricki performed, with few exceptions, only for English-speaking audiences. The design of his extraction exhibition was unlike that of other performers. (Routines and bits of business entered and exited the act. Tricks were added or axed to meet the requirements of time. What I'll describe is his number in its most distilled form.) After an opening salvo of self-deprecating gags ("Let me tell you how to enjoy this. Keep your expectations low."), Rick went into the aisles and brought four fellows up to help. As each was pulled out of his seat, his watch was stolen and held behind the just-chosen helper's back so the audience could clearly see the timepiece. This wordlessly conveyed an unmistakable message: "I'm going to steal things from these fellows, and they'll never catch me doing it. If you watch closely,

Ricki checks every lobby card in Miami to find out where he's working.

you'll see everything I pinch."

With currency borrowed from one of his volunteers, Ricki astonished the audience with the Bill in Lemon. Between greeting the ad hoc committee and discovering the lost bill drowning in lemon juice came twenty solid minutes of gags and deft stealing. His lines were not for the delicate. Holding the arm of one volunteer, he would look toward another and say, "I think I found you a date. Hey, on a foggy night, who's gonna know?" This was humor developed in drinking, smoking, dancing niteries owned by wiseguys where belly laughs were more highly prized than social sensitivity.

The stealing was artfully woven into the magic. Everything Ricki swiped was seen by the audience before being tucked away in his Topit. There were no repeat steals, nor were stolen items returned during the act as misdirection for further thievery. At the end, Rick would race up and down the line of wide-eyed victims returning watches, wallets, a necktie and a belt, proclaiming, "This is the worst night I ever had!"

As the fellows were sent back to their seats, one was asked to stay. He was plopped into a chair, and as the music blared, Rick went into his big-laugh encore. He filled a wine glass with Coke and asked the assistant to gulp it down. Rick had the man tilt his head to the left and he refilled the glass with Coke apparently poured from the fellow's ear. Then liquid was poured from his other ear and his nose. This was all done at Keystone Kops speed. The dazed human fountain was stood up, but before he could escape, Rick grabbed the fellow's collar and pulled his shirt right off from under his jacket. The crowd erupted, and Ricki bowed off to huge laughter show after show on stage after stage for more than thirty years.

Ricki was an excellent technician, but to ensure consistent results he almost always recruited one or more shills even when he wasn't doing the Shirt Pull. On rare occasions he used a *horse* to make certain his shows ran smoothly.

For those with a love of the grifter's patois, Ricki was a revelation. His profanity-laced verbal style (offstage) came from years on carny lots and more years around the broken noses who owned the joints where he plied his trade. He didn't persuade; he "put the arm" on you. He never traveled; he always "made a jump." He didn't do a show; he would "lay down a job." He didn't gain recognition; he "began to make some noise in the business." If you could sing, you "had the box." When Ricki said "costume", he put the emphasis on the second syllable: cos-TUME. The way Ricki pronounced "whore" rhymed with "lure" and came out "whoor".

Ricki's personality was a battleground of contradictions and eccentricities. He was known for his passionate generosity and intensely rough edges. Before Ricki passed away, a wise agent pegged him perfectly, saying, "Ricki Dunn is a true show business character." For more on this paramount variety artist, see *Ricki Dunn: America's No. 1 Pickpocket* by Clarke Crandall (*The New Tops*, December 1963) and *Watch Your Wallets, Hold onto Your Watches! A Remembrance of Ricki Dunn* by David Avadon (*Genii*, July 1999 — see page 93).

Rogues Gallery of Honest Thieves

Performers Around the Globe with a Knack for Nabbing
Imbue the Pickpocket act with their Personal Ingenuity

American Tom Powell, "The Millionaire Pickpocket" (so called because he's stolen millions of dollars during his career), has been emptying pockets for decades. He's one of the few pickpocket entertainers to work college dates fleecing casually dressed students. In his most recent reinvention, he appears before business groups introduced as a maven of whatever their profession happens to be. During his feigned motivational speech, Powell invites spectators on stage for apparently pedagogical purposes, only to have them experiencing withdrawal — from the loss of personal items — in mere minutes.

Performing primarily in Asia, Harry Houdidn't invites spectator after spectator onto the stage for a series of comical, participatory mysteries. Just when the performance seems to be complete, Mr. Houdidn't

Joë Waldys with his assistant Libero.

reaches into his pockets and returns enough loot to stock a pawnshop.

Two mid to late 20th century French wallet removers, Joë Waldys and Patrick Querrot found great success in European nightspots. Waldys, with his male assistant Libero, made use of a butterfly net, the Bra Trick and an Arm Guillotine in his laugh-filled routine. Querrot was part pickpocket, part Gali Gali as he combined his stealing with the production of chicks.

At least two professional dips perform pickpocketing for dummies — actually *with* dummies. Britisher Mark Raffles (Albert Taylor, Jr.) and Frenchman Gérard Majax (Gérard Fater) both perform acts built around a mannequin which suggests a robot or a dressmaker's dummy. (Majax has also used an electrified vest worn by a spectator.) Though the routines are quite different, they have this in common: a lesson in pickpocketing. The obliging pickpocket offers to teach a fellow from the audience the art of lifting wallets. He shows a mannequin wearing a suit coat. He explains that each of the pockets has a bell (or buzzer) attached. He places a wallet in one of the pockets. Then, with the sincerity of a snake oil salesman, he shows that if you remove the wallet swiftly enough, the bell won't ring (or the buzzer buzz), but if you fumble, you'll hear the ringing (or buzzing).

The tutor invites the sucker — er, spectator — to have a go. The poor fellow sets off the noisemaker every time while the instructor's steals are a study in silence. At the end of the lesson, the volunteer student not only fails to fool the bell (buzzer) but realizes that he's been relieved of every personal possession that once filled his pockets. (Mark Raffles has a separate pickpocket routine, sans dummy, built around the cups and chicks.)

Mac Freddy (Holger Wästlund), another fingersmith from Sweden, was content being a successful enchanter of children, content until he saw Dominique in 1956. He was struck by the allure of abstracting and began to imagine an act of his own. In 1959 Dominique came to Stockholm for a two months' stand and needed a translator. Mac Freddy — not Freddie Mac, for those of you in the real estate game — became his Swedish voice. The two became friends and shared professional secrets. In the 1960s, Freddy brought his pickpocketing skills to the United States where he made ten television appearances and was called in as a consultant by the Chicago Police Department.

Born in France, a FISM winner in 1961, Dody Willtohn had ingenious ways of making contact with his audiences. After a series of expert cigarette manipulations, he tossed a handful of monocles into the crowd. Retrieving them provided the misdirection to start his stealing. Eventually he devised a more economical way to motivate his audience invasion. A coin vanished from his fingertips and flew, he was certain, into the pocket of someone in the theater. His search for the coin was his passport to plunder. In the United States, Willtohn has a special notoriety. He was one of the variety acts in Richiardi's World Festival of Magic & Occult which played so successfully to grossed-out crowds at New York's Felt Forum in 1973/74. (Richiardi's performance featured his entrails-splattering version of the buzz saw illusion.)

Two pickpockets share a rare, if obscure, distinction in television history. Jack London (Harold Rifas adopted the stage name Jack London and, although he is better known to conjurers as the author of fine manuscripts on mental magic, he was, as well, a most adept pickpocket)

Jack London on the take.

and Vic Perry both appeared as guests (several years apart) on the hugely popular 1950s game show *What's My Line?*. Their profession: Pickpocket. On the show the celebrity panel's job is to divine the guests' occupations

David Avadon ◈ 51

by asking them a series of questions answered with "yes" or "no." The outcome? London and Perry both stumped the panel! (Vic also appeared on 50s game show favorites *To Tell the Truth* and *I've Got a Secret*.)

Banquets are a venue where entertainers skilled in the five-finger discount can intrigue appreciative audiences. A veteran of many after-dinner shows was Jimmy Ravel, "Mr. Pickpocket." His act had an odd opening. He performed and then taught the audience how to perform the Long and Short Ropes. After that he opened the stage to anyone who cared to join him for some fun. Soon a row of gentlemen stretched the width of the stage looking like a squirming picket fence. The search for a vanished bill gave Ravel the cover he needed to go down the line surreptitiously stealing.

A quick quartet of pocket robbers: Bob Arno from Stockholm, a former assistant to Dominique, picks pockets and removes underwear in nightclubs, on television and at corporate events around the world. American Apollo Robbins sharpened his skills at Caesar's Magical Empire in Las Vegas (an empire which has now vanished). He's equally adept performing for large audiences or for intimate groups of onlookers. Fred and Olly Sylvester from Austria have an unusual distinction: they are team pickpockets. You might call what they do double dipping because both of them do the stealing during their pickpocketing entertainment. It's something they've been doing since the 1950s, and it's taken them to more than forty countries.

"Mr. Pickpocket," Jimmy Ravel.

Unique among performers of this specialty is Henry Kassagi (Abdul Majid Kassaadji). Why? Because of all the dip artists profiled, only Kassagi began life as a real pickpocket on the streets of Tunis and brought his skills from the street to the stage. He became a popular entertainer in France as both pickpocket and

Bertram Otto as Ming Chow.

magician, making many appearances on television. He was featured in the 1959 Robert Bresson film *Pickpocket,* considered by many a masterpiece of French cinema. He played the part of a master *cannon* and also served as technical advisor, fascinating viewers with ingeniously choreographed *touches.*

Audiences love theatricality — exotic costumes, the intrigue of faraway places, grander than life personalities. The English wallet booster Bertram Otto had the most exotic facade of any practitioner ever. Before leaving for an engagement, Otto donned wig, make-up and costume every bit as elaborate as Chung Ling Soo's and emerged from his flat the inscrutable mandarin mystifier Ming Chow, the Light Fingered One. In full regalia, props in hand, he would hail a cab, and head for the exclusive West End hotels where he was in great demand in the 1940s, 50s and 1960s. Imagine the double takes from the English gentry as this celestial being glided through lobbies, down corridors.

After being introduced, he descended into the audience in search of some "sporty-looking chaps and a girl." He returned with six of the first and one of the second. Ming Chow spoke in pidgin English and played everything he did for broad comic effect. He asked the girl if she'd ever seen a Chinese mother in law — then held up a large dragon silk. Each of the volunteers became part of his laugh-provoking sorcery. In the midst of another trick, he suddenly discovered his pockets full of personal property, property expropriated from the unsuspecting helpers. Returning it offered the opportunity for more stealing. One fellow lost his watch even after being forewarned that its theft was imminent. The search for a vanished silk led to the lifting of even more watches, no possessions were sacrosanct. The elusive scarf was finally apprehended far down the back of some poor fellow's trousers.

Mark Raffles, mentioned previously, said that Otto was one the highest-paid, most popular entertainers for posh dinners in the West End of London. Reviewing his act in the *Magic Circular*, one writer enthused, "Ming Chow has the talent to appear outrageously rude to his helpers, but with no offence being taken. There is a warmth and friendliness in his bravura which disarms all hostility, and it is apparent as soon as he walks on that here is a performer of great experience and expertise." Bertram Otto passed away in 1967.

Part-Time Boosters

For many abracadoers, a spot of pickpocketing within a conjuring entertainment both lengthens and brings variety to their performances. Already mentioned were Blackstone, Sr., whose stealthy stealing brought extra fun to his show of a thousand wonders, and Tihany, who used a *horse* in a comic routine of supposed pickpocketing.

John Calvert always included pickpocketing and watch stealing in his full-evening shows. Though better known for large-scale mental feats, David Berglas doubled as a dip. Blackstone, Jr. pretended to fleece his committee with the cooperation of stooges, instant and prepared. Leon Mandrake developed a pickpocket routine as a novelty feature held up his sleeve till needed. Says the supernaturally versatile tricksmeister in *Mandrake Incomparable* (Hades Publications, 1998),

"I once described myself as a professional pickpocket....
I learned to pick pockets as a drop-in specialty of my
various shows." Once caught without props and asked
to perform at a party, Leon launched into his stealing.
Later in an interview the hostess said, "He got my dad up
there and he got his watch, his wallet.... It was incredible
what he did." (The breadth of Mandrake's professional
attainments is "ginormous": ventriloquist, hypnotist,
illusionist, manipulator, mnemonics, mentalism, second
sight, pickpocketing, card scaling, public speaker,
pocket tricks, escape artist, blindfold driver and earthly
incarnation of a comic strip character.)

Another Merlin who broadened the appeal of his
full-evening show with a pickpocket demonstration was
Solimann (Vilheim or Wilhelm Feldvoss, 1885 — 1947)
from Denmark. From the 1920s through the 1940s,
Solimann was the best known mystery attraction in all
of Scandinavia. By 1940 he was Ficktjuvarnas Konung
— King of Pickpockets! (Yes, another Scandinavian and
another pickpocket king!) His routine climaxed with the
discovery of women's intimate apparel in a gentleman's
coat pocket and the production of a large duck from the
same garment.

Always searching for packs-small, plays-big features,
hundreds of magicians have realized that a quiet chat
with a couple of cooperative fellows before a show can
yield five or ten minutes of room-rocking hilarity with
little or nothing in the way of added impedimenta. Instant
cannons, padding their presto with ersatz pickpocketing,

have been a part of conjuring since this specialty act was conceived. Of course, the obvious downside of synthetic stealing is that, in all but the largest venues, word of the bogus modus operandi is certain to leak, leaving disenchantment instead of awe as a lasting impression.

A fine example of nimble pickpocketing well woven into a magical entertainment can be found in the stage show of Paul Potassy. A native of Vienna, Potassy (Ludwig Alexander, 1923 -) survived a Russian prisoner of war camp in World War II to become a most successful nightclub and hotel performer. He dished out comic patter in eight languages — sometimes jumping from language to language during a single show. Sandwiched between the Razor Blades and the Torn and Restored Newspaper came a well-conceived pickpocketing sequence. He evolved a laugh-filled routine which created the maximum impression of skill with the minimum amount of stealing.

One part-time pickpocket who brought histrionics to dipping is the renowned card star John Scarne. Scarne once stole an object of such surpassing importance that the chapter describing the episode was titled "My Greatest Performance" and became the finale of his first autobiography, *The Amazing World of John Scarne: A Personal History* (Crown Publishing, 1956).

In thirteen pages of breathless prose, Scarne describes his experience performing at a party for military leaders in 1944 near the end of World War II. The rodomontade begins with a phone call from Henry "Hap" Arnold,

Commanding General of the United States Army Air Corps, inviting Scarne to perform at a dinner for Sir William Welch, Air Marshal of Great Britain, to be held at the Officers' Club in Bolling Field near Washington D.C. After several pages of anxiety and uncertainty, the nervous Scarne starts his show.

His confidence is restored when the intimate audience of admirals and generals applaud his dexterity. He decides to jazz up his card tricks with some impromptu pocket pinching. He tucks away personal items he's able to lift while producing fans of cards from inside the officers' coats. One of the stolen articles is an envelope. It's thick with folded papers, and Scarne thinks it must be something important. Scarne never reveals the name of the military man from whom he nabbed the envelope. Even more than a decade after the war's end, fearing he could embarrass the officer, he refers to the person only as General X. He reasons that these fellows didn't just meet for dinner and a show. They must have been doing some war-related plan hatching before he arrived — and this envelope could be part of it.

As he returns stolen items, Scarne secretly flashes the envelope to Arnold and whispers that he lifted it from General X. Hap told him, sotto voce, to put it back where he found it — immediately. A humiliating faux pas is avoided when Scarne stealthily returns the envelope before General X ever notices the loss. Hap Arnold appreciated Mr. Scarne's efforts so much he wrote him a lustrous letter of thanks. So what was in this heavy, bulging envelope? Scarne believed it contained part of the Allied plans for the invasion of Japan.

Material World

Artifacts that Reveal the Lore and Lives of Fingersmiths

Y ou might be surprised to learn that writers as diverse as Ed Marlo and U.F. Grant have written about pickpocketing. Ed Marlo's *How to Remove a Wrist Watch* (Magic Inc., n.d.) has suggestions for stealing watches — particularly those of other magicians. If you are U.F. Grant and you have a blank sheet of paper and an hour to kill, you start typing and, sixty minutes later, you have fifteen ideas (both original and borrowed) for pseudo pickpocketing called *Pickpocketing Stunts* (self-published, n.d.).

Develop your linguistic skills by reading about pickpockets in other languages. Spanish: A teaching tome called *Pick Pocket* by Eddie and Roger (CYMYS, 1975). Swedish: Theatrical pickpockets are profiled in *Trollare* by Christer Nilsson (Spektra, n.d.). German: Alexander Adrion pens a panorama of pickpocketing in *Taschendiebe* (C.H. Beck, 1993), with brief stories of pickpockets on the street, on the stage, and in films and literature. (I was especially charmed by the name of one female cannon: Lady Finger.)

For those interested in learning the techniques of the *touch*, here are three pickpocket primers: *The Pickpocket Secrets of Mark Raffles* by Mark Raffles (The Magic Box, 1982); *Complete Course in Pick Pocketing* by Pierre Jacques (previously cited); *Jim Ravel's Theatrical Pickpocketing* by Paul Butler (Magical Publications, 1988). But keep this caution in mind: Pickpocketing and bull riding are two very difficult things to learn from a book. Both are visceral activities made up of physical sensations impossible to communicate in words. And both involve close contact with unpredictable creatures. What these courses in pickpocketing include is helpful, but what they lack is crucial. Absent from every text is instruction in how to discover one's "pickpocket persona," the theatrical personality which will allow the performer to reliably cover his steals with convincing misdirection. Missing from every book is the concept of rhythm and pace, the necessity of developing a wave of inevitability in the act which carries volunteers smoothly through the routine by offering them the path of least resistance. And the most important omission from every course of instruction is how to give the steals a context, how to make every steal an organic part of a larger theatrical construction.

One book which does address these issues in a helpful

Mark Raffles, author of The Pickpocket
Secrets of Mark Raffles *and* Diamond
Jubilee Memoirs.

way is *Hey! That's My Wallet!* by Walt Hudson (Magic Media Ltd., 1978). This slim, ten-page manuscript details the author's pseudo-pickpocket act done with two stooges — exactly the kind of act I railed against earlier. But because it is a *routine* instead of a collection of individual steals, and, because the author stresses the theatrical elements which make the routine both comical and convincing, the reader comes away with insights into the elements necessary to frame any style of pickpocket turn.

The Professional Stage Pickpocket by Ricki Dunn (Nielsen Magic, 2006) is the finest of all the teaching texts. Ricki was one of the premiere pickpockets of the twentieth century both as a technician and a showman. Before he passed away in 1999, he spent two years carefully recording all of his methods and routines. Here a beginner will learn to give the illusion of pickpocketing while developing genuine skills. Advanced students will learn the ingenious strategies Ricki used to accomplish the most difficult steals and prevail under the most daunting performing conditions. Ricki teaches the paramount lesson of the stage pickpocket, something even more important than the technical tricks of the taking trade: every steal is connected to misdirection, misdirection is an organic part of the act and the act comes from the unique personality of the performer. (Note: Unfortunately, this book is marred by the absence of thoughtful editing. Poorly written sentences and inaccurately described techniques detract from what would have been a superb teaching text.)

Pickpockets, nimble fingers in high gear, pop up on television, sometimes as performers and sometimes exposing the ways of their street-thieving, pocket-picking cousins. They can be seen on talk shows, variety shows and programs devoted to travel and self-help. Those quick on the record button can capture these performances on VCRs and TIVO.

Are you a film buff? Pickpocketing sequences occur in motion pictures as diverse as *The Maltese Falcon*

(1941), *Lifeboat* (1944) and *Gangs of New York* (2002) — three from hundreds of movies with touches of *touches* in them. These cinematic depictions almost always disregard the actions necessary for actually copping wallets. One that I can't resist mentioning is *Heartbeat* (1946). In it Basil Rathbone plays the demonic dean of a school for pickpockets. In his classroom there is a stroke of memorable, big-screen imagination: it's a merry-go-round of mannequins in suit coats. As the dummies fly by at an ever faster pace, the students have only nanoseconds to make their steals. The concept is equally ridiculous and inspired.

Some films, like the previously mentioned *Pickpocket*, intrigue viewers with a realistic, if stylized, delineation of pickpocket ploys. The *Great Train Robbery* (1979) contains a cleverly staged I-dare-you-to-catch-the-pickpocket-at-work sequence. While showing the activity on a London street, a whiz mob robs a young lady. Though the crime is performed in full view and we're introduced in advance to the perpetrators, the misdirection is so powerful that viewers in the theater never notice the *touch* till they are "put wise" and the scene is replayed. *Harry in Your Pocket* (1973) follows two recruits as they learn the ways of the *wire mob* and features pickpocketing sequences cleverly choreographed by technical advisor Tony Giorgio.

Writing Wrongs

Several years ago in Chicago, I listened as a magician proudly deconstructed one of Borra's techniques for me. The secret, he confided, had been revealed to him by a well-known mentalist who had seen the light-fingered Serbian and sussed his M.O. What he shared as gospel was so screwy I had to bite my cheek to keep from laughing. Like mentalists, writers can be mistaken too. I'd like to correct some painful errors in print so readers and writers alike have a more accurate picture of pickpocket performers.

Geschichte der Zauberkunst, Dr. Kurt Volkmann, 1957. (This is an obscure reference for American readers, but it has been used by other researchers.)

As part of a series of articles on the history of magic, Dr.

Volkmann wrote a paragraph on the origins of theatrical pickpocketing. He mistakenly gives Dr. Giovanni's date of birth as 1876 and the date of his death as 1954 in Rio de Janeiro. Dr. Giovanni died in 1977 in Los Angeles. According to the *Los Angeles Times* story noting his passing, he was born in 1896. Volkmann's overview also contains misdated references to articles in the *Linking Ring*.

The Complete Professional Pickpocket, David Alexander, 1979.

The book includes an interview with someone who claimed to have worked as a stooge (*horse*) for Dominique. Based on the information offered by the supposed ex-employee, Alexander concludes that there was no genuine pickpocketing in Dominiques's act. Actually, real pickpocketing commingled with the pretend. The assistant chosen for the Bill in Cigarette was not stooged; the steals were genuine. The former confederate gives a completely incorrect explanation of what happened when Dominique went through the audience stealing articles. Dominique only needed to lift two or three things during this tour and the steals were done legitimately. The problem is with David's informant. This must have been someone who had seen Dominique's show but never really worked for him. Dominique didn't use paid stooges, he only used confederates recruited from the audience, and he made it a strict rule to never use the same person twice.

In a section on street pickpockets, Alexander describes the School of the Bells where students learn to lift a wallet without ringing bells attached to a coat. Sound familiar? The existence of the school is a myth, but a myth that even law enforcement experts believe. At one police lecture I attended, a bunco squad officer explained that graduates of the School of the Bells were given a special tattoo and an identifying ring. A street pickpocket would never have anything that would mark him as a dip. Alexander describes another school that outfits all of its graduates with a disguise consisting of a raincoat, hat, horn-rimmed glasses and a black attache case. Nonsense. Think how wonderfully easy that would make it for police officers to spot these alumni, all in the same threads. (I'm sure David was repeating stories gleaned from police manuals. As I said earlier, policemen are not pickpockets.)

Conjuring, James Randi, St. Martin's Press, 1992.

Describing Dr. Giovanni, Randi writes, "He was a substantial gentleman, and used to advertise that he traveled with '300 kilos of baggage' but that most of the weight was his own body." He has almost certainly confused Giovanni with Vic Perry. I have films of Giovanni in the 1930s and the 1950s, and I knew him in the 1970s. Though his powerful showmanship made him seem larger than life on stage, he was, in fact, slight and wiry. Randi goes on to say that Giovanni "traveled with his entire family in attendance, along with appropriate tutors." His "entire family" could only have been his wife and, rarely, his daughter with possibly a nursemaid to care for her. Hardly the entourage Randi describes.

Randi mentions Borra stealing belts. Borra stole suspenders, never belts. Referring to volunteers, he says, "Of course, their watches are in Borra's pockets before they even take their seats onstage." Randi may be thinking of Ricki Dunn, who lifted spectators' watches as he brought them out of their seats. Borra did an impressive routine of twice stealing the watch of the first fellow he invited up. He never did additional watch steals after that.

Describing Borra, Randi says, "There are two Borra brothers who are also doing the act." Borra told me that his brothers died in World War II, but the precise facts are elusive. A performer billed as Borra II performed at The China Theatre in Stockholm in July 1952. Without question, though, neither of Borra's brothers survived into the 1990s as Randi suggests.

Finally, two small spelling corrections: According to Charlie Borra's web site, it's "Charlie," not "Charly," and Gentleman Jack's student is "Kenny Quinn," not "Kenny Queen."

Dramatic Magic, John Booth, Ridgeway Press, 1988.

Booth describes meeting Vic Perry in Chicago during the

1930s. Perry would only have been a teenager in England at the time. I believe this is a typo and should have been the 1950s. He goes on to say, "Vic Perry's act revolved around the Miser's Dream." Although Perry *said* he was going to find coins in spectators' clothing, none was produced as he went from fellow to fellow rifling pockets. Booth also says that Perry used an "under-jacket bag." I can't say that Perry never used a Topit during his career, but he did not use one in any of the shows I saw. He stashed all the stolen items in his own commodious pockets.

"Borra: King of Pickpockets," John Fisher, *Genii*, March 1996.

The author makes the case that Borra was the only pickpocket who didn't use magic tricks as misdirection for his steals. He writes, "More relevant is the fact that all the leading ... pickpockets [i.e. all except Borra] use magic as an incidental cover to distract the attention of their subjects ..." He then gives some examples: "Dominique with his Electric Chairs" "Vic Perry and the Miser's Dream" "Even Giovanni used the Ring on Stick in this way ..."

It's true the Electric Chairs were part of Dominique's performance, but the routine was not part of the pickpocketing and wasn't used as a misdirection for dipping. Had he said the Bill in Cigarette, that would have been accurate, since one stealing sequence was built around that effect. However, he was completely mistaken about Vic Perry and Dr. Giovanni. In Perry's case, the suggestion that coins would be produced gave him a pretext to go into the audience and do some preliminary nicking. But once the men were on the stage, there were no more props and no more magic tricks. It was pickpocketing, pure and skillful. With Giovanni, the Ring on Stick didn't shade his stealing. (There was one charming piece of business he used occasionally as part of this trick. After showing that he could push a borrowed ring onto the center of the stick, the next time the ring went through he had a surprise waiting. When he pulled his hand away, instead of the ring spinning on the stick, it was a previously stolen watch.) The magic tricks Giovanni performed were performance pieces in between his wallet importing expeditions.

Even I'm not immune from unintentional gaffs. Writing about Borra in the January 1997 issue of *Magic*, I said that he had never appeared in the Ringling Brothers' Circus. According to Dominique he did, if only briefly. Since this was a three ring circus, performances in the outer two rings had to be halted while Borra worked in the center. At such a great distance, patrons at the far ends of the arena just couldn't see what he was doing. After a few shows, Borra and the circus management agreed it wasn't working. Borra went to England to appear in the Bertram Mills Circus where he became a great star for many years.

The Art of the Steal

It is astonishing that not one pickpocket is profiled in the two most widely read one-volume histories of magic: Milbourne Christopher's *Illustrated History of Magic* (Thomas Y. Crowell Company, 1973) and David Price's *Magic: A Pictorial History of Conjurers in the Theater* (Cornwall Books, 1985). (To be scrupulous, Dominique is accorded a seven-word mention, one of which is his name, in the Christopher book.)

Christopher limns portraits of quick-change artists, regurgitators and learned horses, but doesn't give a nod to Dr. Giovanni or Borra who, between them, created the canon of theatrical *cannons*. David Price didn't like hypnotists, but he devoted pages to profiling the most successful of these vaudeville Svengalis. Pages for hyp acts, but not the briefest mention of a pickpocket. Where's Dominique who reimagined the stage pickpocket and became one of the most crowd-pleasing attractions in nightclub showrooms around the world? I don't mean to rattle a saber at these authors. Their omission reflects the blind spot rabbit tuggers feign when a pickpocket takes the stage. They just don't see him.

Actually, I think it's more than just pickpocket-proof shutters. When unsophisticated magicians see a performer whose act is built entirely on nerve and bravado and they sense high-flying skill they could never match, they're intimidated. The insecure respond with resentment. After all, once you've seen an audience clap their hands raw for a wallet-stealing swashbuckler, suddenly making one tassel grow longer while the other becomes shorter doesn't seem so grand. Tricksters without wise insight into their own branch of conjuring choose to ignore these crowd-wowing showmen. To them, a pickpocket is a black sheep in a tux.

And that's a raw deal. Why? Because, to be as clear as possible, a pickpocket is a magician, a magician with a specialty act. Exhibition pickpockets are magicians drawn to bravura burglary as other magicians are attracted to illusions, escapes, manipulation or mentalism. Many pickpockets (Dody Willtohn, Borra, Gentleman Jack, Dominique) begin their performances with deft sleight-of-hand arabesques. Often these theatrical thieves (Dr. Giovanni, Ricki Dunn, Dominique, Jöe Waldys) build their acts around superbly routined tricks. Dominique and Dody Willtohn were, as I mentioned, FISM competitors. Borra, in his seventies when I met him, showed me coin manipulation that was strikingly original and surpassingly difficult. Arise, fellow wizards, your vision fully restored.

Shirts that Pull

Now let us speak of many things, of stooges, shills and shirts that pull. Is it right or wrong to tip your mit to some of the civilians so that all the rest think you are the King of Pickpockets? Is the tidal wave of laughs and the illusion of super-stealthy skill worth the jarring chorus of tattletales left behind? It's a question wrestled with not only by pickpockets but by magicians, mentalists — even close-up chaps. Here's a jumble of relevant anecdotes and observations.

Dominique recruited enough stooges to field a baseball team for every show he did and was regarded as one of the greatest showroom attractions of his era. Blackstone, Jr. couldn't steal a watch for all the thumb tips in China, but the illusion of pickpocketing was a big feature in the routine he inherited from his father, the Committee. Instant stooging served the Blackstone family well for two generations. Often magicians, even savvy veterans, can't spot a well-hidden plant. Many people have recollected for me the time they saw a pickpocket steal a man's shirt right off his back, to them a never-forgotten wonder. An equal number of people have told me they spotted the act for a fake the moment the shirt came off. No amount of skill, they realized, could swipe a shirt, collar first. When Giovanni moved to Los Angeles, his calendar filled with club dates. One local agent tried for years to get him to do the Shirt Pull because it was such a huge laugh-getter with every audience. No sale. On the other hand, Ricki Dunn told me that he counted on the Shirt Pull to put him over in the rowdy night clubs where he was first employed and developed *sells* to convince club owners the stunt was legit. More average Joes than I can remember have told me about the time they were taken backstage by Blackstone, Jr. (or other well-know pickpockets) and prepped for the shirt gag.

In a grand Las Vegas review, I watched a pickpocket whose act depended on two carefully prepared audience members. As I was leaving the showroom, I saw a crowd of people gathered around one of the pickpocket's volunteers. In response to their quizzing, he divulged every particular of his backstage coaching. Then I saw another cluster of people. They were huddled around the other helper. And *he* was dishing out all the details of *his* pre-show initiation. Stereophonic whistle blowers!

Ricki Dunn was an excellent technician, well capable of smooth pickpocketing without a single plant, but he used stooges in nearly every show he did. This was his philosophy: When you're hired to do a show, the booker wants to hear the same in-the-aisles laughter and see the same tremendous reactions that got you the job to begin with. He has no interest in how you do your act; he's paying for a result. Your job, reasoned Ricki, is to deliver by the most foolproof means possible.

I've never seen a pickpocket in a major Las Vegas review who didn't rely on confederates. Casino bosses want reviews to run exactly the ninety minutes allotted them so marks return to the tables right on schedule. If a variety act is given ten minutes, they expect it to run ten minutes — and no seconds. Easy if you're a manipulator working to music; impossible if you're a pickpocket with a stage full of punters who may or may not fall instantly under your spell.

Where a thousand people or more are mostly strangers to one another, a pickpocket who takes out insurance with plants and *horses* can go undetected. But in any other setting, the real thing has a big advantage. Performing for business groups or organizations, try to pass off a *horse*, and they'll know instantly he's not with the company. Set up a few sports for big sight gags, and no matter how solemnly they've been sworn to secrecy, they're certain to blab to their co-workers. There is nothing that sells a pickpocket act — in any venue — like the genuine shock of surprise. When a cannon returns a wallet to someone who can't believe it was stolen, the gent's reaction sells the pickpocket's skill to everyone else in the room. And when groups chat after the show, the performer's reputation soars when helpers swear to their total amazement.

Here's the show business law of the jungle: If a sure-enough pickpocket wants to compete with a "Take-your-watch-off-and-hold-it-behind-your-back" guy, he has to be able to match the other performer laugh for laugh, gasp for gasp, show after show. Challenging — but not impossible!

If you think of yourself as a judge in the Olympic pickpocketing competition, what do you look for? How do you assess what you've seen? Like mindreading and hypnotic acts, pickpocketing is framed for the tastes of laymen, and the key is to see the act through the eyes of the paying customers. When the lifting, nicking and pinching is for real, watch the volunteers on stage. Are they having a jolly time, or do they look like they've been shanghaied? Are they genuinely amazed when the wallet wizard produces their belongings, or do their expressions say, "I'll take that back if you're through with it"? How does the showman handle a contretemps? Are you seeing a routine that's fresh, with steals that are daring and adroit?

But if you're watching a fingersmith who uses enough plants to start a rain forest, *then* how do you rate what you're seeing? You judge it like you would a play. Do you believe the actors — pickpocket and victims alike? Is the counterfeit stealing plausible? Are the bits of business ingenious? Are they original? Does the performer extract the greatest comic effect from every situation? Are you swept away and thoroughly entertained by the act? Again, watch the audience, see it through their eyes.

Paul Potassy, mentioned earlier, had some well-reasoned rules that governed what he did in his act. He never held a stolen item over the victim's head for the audience to see. He never swiped a belt or a tie. Paul felt these bits of business made the spectator look foolish. Audiences can tell instantly whether the performer is there to take unfair advantage of well-meaning volunteers or to entertain with a fascinating skill.

Dr. Freud to the Stage, Please

Magic, mentalism, escapes, hypnosis and pickpocketing each touch the most elemental human desires. Magic — to have supernatural control over the physical world, to escape the bounds of gravity, to make the dead rise. Mentalism — to know the private thoughts of another human being. Escapes — to free oneself from any form of imprisonment. Hypnosis — to make a person helpless to resist one's every command. Pickpocketing, too, invokes a powerful primal impulse — to take a man's possessions right off his body while one is unseen and unsuspected.

Pickpocketing is the ultimate expression of passive-aggressive behavior. It is anger and rage sublimated to invisibility. It is a show of power over another man by taking his valuables (an intentional double entendre) and leaving him clueless. It is to make a boob of another man with one's superior stealth and cunning. These are the primitive emotions conjured up, albeit subconsciously, by every act of pocket stealing.

On a conscious level, audiences relate to a pickpocket the way they would to a magician doing the Paper Balls Over the Head, Powers of Darkness or the Card on the Forehead. They see his performance as a fascinating exhibition of adroit skill and spectacular misdirection. The volunteers on stage will feel that way too, given the right balance of respectful treatment and spirited fun, even though they're the ones who've lost their wallets.

It is in our nature to fantasize about committing a crime undetected. The more daring the crime, the greater the thrill. Viewing a master pickpocket, the audience experiences vicariously a crime spree of breathtaking audacity. Spectators marvel as the fingersmith steals thousands of dollars in cash, credit cards and jewelry. A pickpocket act can be a superbly satisfying example of wish fulfillment as entertainment.

Turn wish fulfillment inside out and you have fear. That, too, is part of the allure of exhibition pickpocketing. Each of us can imagine how miserable it would be to have our cash stripped, our identities ripped off and our credit cards exploited by a rat-faced pickpocket on the street. But put that fear at a comfortable distance, up on the stage, and dread is morphed into a socially affable experience: entertainment.

Do pickpockets get caught? All the time, even the best in the world. Pickpocketing is the human-to-human

activity which most closely resembles a bullfight. The implied contest between the cannon and the mark — the cannon pitting his speed and slyness against the mark's natural desire not to be robbed and not to be made a fool of — provides the emotional tension in a performance of exhibition pickpocketing.

I have no ear for jazz, no eye for modern art. Others feel the same "I don't get it" when a cannon takes the stage. The excitement of the pickpocket's improvisational tightrope-walk is lost on some people — and some audiences as well. There are settings — in front of urchins and octogenarians, for example — where a demonstration of clever stealing is destined to thud. But where the syzygy of performer, crowd and venue exists, the joint is jumpin'!

Much is written about "meaning" in magic. Magicians fret over what it is and how to create it. "Why," they moan, "can't a magic show have the emotional impact of a great film?" The result of this *Sturm und Drang*? Not much. Examples of "meaning" put forward are routines with more treacle than poignancy, theme acts with more novelty than art. I believe that meaning can't be scripted, that it comes from an unexpected convergence of artist, audience and moment. It comes with the performer's ability to recognize the uniqueness of a fleeting speck of time and shape his number to the circumstance. For the right customers under the right conditions, even the comic antics of a pickpocket can have unexpected depth.

From the 1948 *Esquire* article cited earlier, here's how Arnold Gingrich described the significance of Borra's skills in post-World War II Vienna: "His...preferred victim for this culminating point in his performance is...a Russian in uniform. For even now, over two years after the wild nightmare of the Red Army's orgy of 'liberation,' the sight of somebody taking a watch away from a Russian is the Viennese equivalent of seeing a man bite a dog. ...[E]very time Borra [gets] one of them out on the floor and begins looting him...you can sense...that in the eyes of the breathlessly watching Viennese this...debonair young man is acquiring heroic stature of...mythical proportion."

Fin

That's the theatrical pickpocket from criminal roots to murky beginnings, from show business dawning to heroic potential. This is an appreciation of magical performers brave enough to shed their props and create bold entertainment relying on dash, showmanship, misdirection and humor.

Though the objects in pockets will change and the clothing to which those pockets are attached will transform in unimagined ways, audiences will forever gasp in admiration at swift-fingered charmers who entertain by extraction.

Editorial Perspective

This is one history of exhibition pickpocketing. Additional histories from many vantage points could easily be written. This monograph is limited in scope; otherwise, a stage full of equally worthy pickpocket entertainers not mentioned would certainly have been included.

Acknowledgments

I gratefully acknowledge the generous help of everyone listed below. Their expert assistance with research, translation and editorial guidance transformed the work you've read. I'd like to add that, to many of these people, I was a complete stranger when I approached them for aid, and that they would so freely offer their time and learning is something I deeply appreciate. To all of you my grateful, grateful thanks: Francisco Aparicio, Gordon Bean, Leo Behnke, Mathieu Bich, Edwin A. Dawes, Sid Fleischman, Ethel Gullette, Richard Hatch, Ingrid Herzer, Joe Herzer, Volker Huber, Marilyn Kass, David Meyer, Christer Nilsson, Mary Parrish, Dominique Risbourg, Peter Schuster, Adolfo Valvaroza, and Wittus Witt.

Profiles in
Pickpocketing

Watch your Wallets, Hold on to your Watches!
A Remebrance of Ricki Dunn

A belt slithers snake-like from a spectator's pants. A necktie flys from another man's shirt. The one-liners come out faster than a boxer's combination punch. High-energy music kicks in. The white-haired performer reaches into his coat and pulls out handfuls of items swiped from the on-stage helpers. The dumbfounded volunteers realize their watches and wallets are gone and quickly check their pockets to see what else might be missing. Roaring laughter drowns out the music. Suddenly the act is over, the performer returns for a bow, the applause is deafening, and the walls of the theater turn to Jell-O. This was Ricki Dunn tearing up a audience as no one else could. This was "America's Funniest Pickpocket" at his best. And now, much too soon, he's gone.

Ricki fused two theatrical elements never blended

Ricki Dunn, America's Funniest Pickpocket.

before. He took the European pickpocket act as pioneered by Dr. Giovanni and linked it with cutting edge night club humor. The result was alchemy. He evolved one of the classic acts in magic, as powerful and individual in its genre as any act in show business. In the 1950s when only the merest number of magicians could find work in nightclubs, Ricki's high voltage pickpocket turn kept him solidly booked, in great demand. In fact, he kept his date book full for more than thirty years, a record very few professionals could match.

He was the most successful performer you've never read about in a magic magazine. I've taken the stories Ricki shared with me over the twenty years I knew him and shaped them into a portrait. I've done this mostly for myself so I wouldn't forget the yarns he spun as we drove together or chatted (Rick would say "cut up jackpots") in restaurants. If you never met Ricki or only saw him on stage, get ready to have your eyes opened. Meet a show business lion with a personality as complex as the branches in a monkey puzzle tree.

Dr. Giovanni was one of the first conjurers to build an act entirely around pickpocketing. In the 1930's and 40's he was the most famous dip artist in the United States and Great Britain. When Giovanni retired to Beverly Hills in the 1960s for a life of golf and occasional club dates, Ricki was reaching his peak as a performer. He became the most prominent pickpocket in America and one of the most financially successful variety artists in the country.

Born on April 2nd, Ricki Dunn began life as Freddy Revello, a stocky kid from a poor Italian family in Newark, New Jersey. Magic fascinated the youngster. One day a friend showed him a crude second deal. Rick was practicing the move on the stairway outside the family's apartment when his father came home. His dad was a professional gambler. (Rick described him as someone who made money playing cards so he could throw it away at the track.) "Hey, pop," said Ricki, "look at this," and the little guy enthusiastically demonstrated his new skill. His dad watched him perform the painfully rough sleight and said, "Look, if you're gonna do that, at least learn to do it right." Then he sat down on the steps with the boy and took the time to show him the finer points of second dealing. Rick said it was the one fond memory he had of his father.

Every summer a carnival played near Ricki's home. At fourteen, he gathered up his meager bag of tricks (the most impressive of which was the 20th Century Silks) and tried to get a job on the lot. When a show operator took him on (Rick lied and said he was 16), that was the end of Ricki's formal education and the beginning of his life as a carny. For the next several years he was "with it," working in carnivals all over the country. He learned to eat fire and to juggle — a skill which he could perform atop a tightrope while balanced on one foot. While at Chicago's Riverview Park, he was billed as "The Torture King" and laid down on a bed of nails he built himself. The engagement ended in a fist fight with the owner, a negotiating technique Rick was to employ on numerous occasions.

He mastered carny skills and he soaked up carny speech, along with some, but not many, of the carny's bad habits. Rick never smoked, and he always said that his next drink would be his first. Between carnival stints, he returned to his home in New Jersey. The local teens in his working class neighborhood would needle him about not smoking which was de rigueur among his peers. His response was to take out his torches, blow some impressive blasts of flame, and say, "Do you really think I have to smoke a cigarette to prove how tough I am?" When his hooligan friends belittled him because he wouldn't take a drink, he had an equally powerful, typically Ricki, and thoroughly unprintable reply.

Rick's stories of his carnival years were liberally peppered with sultry tales of the young women he met while crisscrossing the country. (Actually, all of Rick's stories, carnival or otherwise, were liberally peppered with — .)

In those early years, Rick would dare any idea that jumped into his head. While working as a clown on an auto thrill show, he convinced the owners to allow him to perform an extra attraction. What was the stunt? He claimed he could escape from a straight jacket while being dragged around the track by a rope attached to the back of a speeding race car. And he did it — once.

He worked for a time as an assistant on the Card Mondor spook show "Dracula's Den of Living

Nightmares" where he met Dick Newton who would become a lifelong friend. Ricki's job the first night was to close the curtains at a crucial moment in the show. While he waited in the wings, Card's statuesque wife, Donna, a voluptuous blond, oozed onto the stage wrapped in a dressing gown. A stunning showgirl, she was billed as "Six Feet Six Inches of 'HEX' Appeal." She entered a cabinet, the front of which had a window shade which was pulled down. A spotlight at the back of the cabinet made her every move visible in silhouette on the shade. She removed her robe in a most tantalizing way, then — and this was really hot for the 1940s — she peeled off her bra and her panties. Rick was mesmerized, lost in a powerful sexual reverie. As she bent to raise the shade, the spotlight went out. When the shade flew up, the nude woman had become a gorilla which charged into the audience scaring the hell out of the teenagers. The curtains were to close immediately behind the gorilla, but that night they never closed at all. Backstage Ricki went slack jawed when the stark naked (she wore a body suit, but who knew), gorgeous bombshell rushed past him. He was frozen, motionless, in awe.

The dubious glamour of carnival life paled, and, in his late teens, Ricki moved to New York in search of work as a magician. He discovered work was not in search of him. Lou Tannen befriended Rick and hired him from time to time to do small jobs. Ricki once accepted a date performing close-up with several other magicians at a large banquet. He was assigned to work the balcony area of this hall — but couldn't muster the courage to approach a single table. Instead, he ducked out the back and headed for Tannen's. Three hours later he reappeared and lined up with the other magicians to collect his check. As the fellow handed him his fee, Rick said, "Boy, it sure was hot up there." These were lean times for Rick, but things were about to change.

Bruce Elliott took a liking to Ricki. He allowed him to attend the Friday night, back-room sessions he hosted, informal meetings which attracted the premiere sleight-of-hand performers and magical thinkers of the day. At that time Ricki was doing what he described as a "half-assed comedy act." (According to Ray Goulet, it was heavily influenced by Roy Benson's work.) But he wanted to find something that would be uniquely his own. One night Elliott's back-room bunch began to talk about what kind of an act would be best for Ricki, and someone (Ricki told Clarke Crandall the idea came from Lou Tannen) tossed out: pickpocket. Nods of approval went 'round the room. Rick was instantly taken with the notion. Dr. Jaks was one of the group, and he shared with Ricki everything he knew about the European pickpockets he had seen.

He put together his first routine ("framed the act"), and, after backing down several times, found the nerve to try it on an out-of-town date. Not great — yet — but he sensed this was "the way to go." When Rick pursued something he wanted, he was ferocious. Convinced the act was right for him, he was unstoppable. He became totally focused on perfecting his act. No amount of effort was too much when he was tracking down moves and gags that might fit in. He convinced friends to let him practice his steals on them for hours at a time. He attached himself to the police detective in charge of the pickpocket squad so he could learn how street dips operated. If he had an idea for a prop, he spent any amount of money necessary to have it made.

Rick's closest friends in New York were Norman Jensen, Howard Brooks and Robert Orben. Bob was a constant help in these struggling years, not only with gags and bits of business, but with endless encouragement — and even a ride to the gig when he needed it.

His doggedness began to pay off. Work started to come his way. As Rick put it, he "began to make some noise in the business." As the neon in Rick's star flickered on, the Palace Theater was bringing back vaudeville. Every magician in town wanted a chance to "play the Palace." One of the few who got the nod during the short-lived revival was Ricki Dunn.

Early reviews from the nightspots he played described him as a "whirlwind." What Rick had fashioned was a turn perfectly suited to the nightclub scene of the 1950s. *Variety* called him "fast", "furious" and "funny." And he was in demand — everywhere! The Elmwood Casino in Windsor, the 500 Club in Atlantic City, the Town Casino in Buffalo, the Horizon Room in Pittsburg, the Holiday House in Milwaukee, Suttmiller's in Dayton, the Playboy Club in Chicago. In an era when only a handful of magicians could find work in nightclubs, Ricki was

Ricki commences to rock the house. (The seated woman is for his version of the Bra Trick. See The Professional Stage Pickpocket *by Ricki Dunn.)*

booked 52 weeks out of the year.

In the mid-1950s, he followed his friend Howard Brooks to Miami where Ricki appeared in reviews at every major hotel and wowed conventioneers at banquet shows. Miami attracted scores of top entertainers. Rick struck up friendships with many of them, including Barclay Shaw. In pre-Castro Cuba, he performed several times in Havana. During the day he was recognized in the street by Cubans who'd seen his show, and was followed by crowds who'd heard of his marvelous feats.

In the early 60s he moved on to Chicago and quickly became one of the workingest fellows in the city. When it came to improving his act and promoting himself, Ricki was indefatigable. He had sessions with other comics and magicians during which they brainstormed gags and lines for each other's acts. (One struggling newcomer who asked the group for help was Harry Blackstone, Jr. Rick offered invaluable material, a kindness which later led to another of Ricki's blazing brawls.) He came up with clever ideas for gifts which he gave to the agents who booked him. He had an ad in *Variety* which ran continuously. It read simply: "Ricki Dunn is a thief!" George Johnstone, Mike Caldwell and Senator Crandall were some of his many windy city pals.

Though he was one of the most commercially successful performers in the country, you'd never know it by reading magician's trade journals. He only once made the cover of a magic magazine: The December 1963 issue of *The New Tops*, which featured an article about Ricki by Clarke Crandall.

Las Vegas had shows too, big ones, and Ricki began to work in them. The Flamingo, the Aladdin, the Dunes and the Hacienda all featured Ricki in their reviews. Looking for volunteers one night, Rick spotted Elvis in the audience and managed to lift the crooner's watch.

After Las Vegas, Rick spent many years performing almost exclusively on cruise ships. Instead of two shows a night, he only had to do two shows per cruise. Members

The Hot Seats' victim leaps from his chair.

of the cruise staff sported tags with their name and position. Ricki's read "Ricki Dunn: Thief." Audiences on the ships and Ricki's act were a perfect match; the work was steady and the years slipped by.

It wasn't until well into the 1980s that worked lessened for Ricki ("white space in the date book"), and that was after three decades of solid bookings. He still did nightclubs (Magic Island, The Magic Castle, Wizardz), cruise ships, tours (with Chuck Jones and Bob Kenney), television spots and club dates, but he began to do them more occasionally.

Ricki constantly toyed with ideas for tricks and gags. Some of them are now standard effects which can be found in dealers' catalogs. As a kid he experimented with blindfold methods, and he worked up a handling that was so good he sold the idea to Lou Tannen. You'll find it in the Tannen catalog under the moniker Sightless Vision. In the 1950s, he considered doing a dove act on ice skates for an ice revue. His experiments led to the invention of the Dove Streamer, major improvements in the Double Dove Production Bag, and the development of the Gloves to Dove production tray. (Fortunately, Rick came to his senses before stepping out onto the ice.) He had the original idea which became Al Cohen's Shogun Wallet. A few years ago, while looking at a 3 1/2 of clubs card, he realized there was a better way to lay out the pips so audiences could more quickly grasp the humorous incongruity. He had several hundred printed, and they were quickly snapped up by savvy dealers who appreciated the improvement.

Ricki twice offered his notions in book form. In the 60s, when a campy version of *Batman* became a huge hit on television, he wrote *Bat Magic*, a collection of tricks and gags themed to the popular show. *Zapped!* was his exploration of the Hot Seats revealing every piece of business in his repertoire.

You'd hardly call Rick a philosopher, but, in a lifetime spent entertaining, he formed some opinions worth careful consideration:

•Early on, he found a piece of advice in *The Sphinx* which he considered so strikingly valuable that he committed the lines to memory. The writer suggested that magicians study the very best singers, dancers and entertainers, study their pacing, their staging and the excitement they generated, because if a magician is to find a place on the stage, reasoned the writer, he must be able to compete with these slick stars.

•Magicians who saw Ricki for the first time later in his career were sometimes put off by his rough brand of humor. Rick was not a refined artiste delighting genteel patrons. He was from another era. His act was forged in raucous, boozy nightclubs. He shared the stage with sexy dancers and ribald comedians, and his banter was dictated by the taste of the clientele. Rick was often criticized for the put-down humor in his act. Examples: To a volunteer not following Rick's instructions fast enough: "Did you see that? He damn near moved." Fingering a gentleman's coat: "Is this that new material — Styrofoam?" Talking to one man while pointing to another: "I think I found you a date. Hey, on a foggy night, who's gonna know." His own point of view on comedy, though, was fascinating. He believed that if you call a bald man "bald" or a fat man "fat," *that* was put-down humor; but the lines that he used were obviously not personally directed at the men on stage and were, therefore, not offensive. They were

The audience roars as Ricki returns the loot he's lifted on what he would call "the worst night I ever had!"

simply lines. In fact, they were gags the spectators tried to remember so they could use these quips themselves.

•Though some would call Rick's material heavy handed (ex.: When giving a spectator the corner from a torn bill: "That's the only piece you're gonna get tonight"), there was one type of comedy he never used: bathroom humor. Rick considered toilet humor the most repugnant form of comedy. It was never part of his act nor of his amazingly large repertoire of jokes.

•A well-meaning magician once complimented Ricki on his effective use of stooges. Rick thanked him with a punch in the face. (Really!) He always insisted, even to his closest friends, that he never used stooges. But, of course, he did. He used confederates for the Shirt-Pull and the Hot Seats, and, on certain shows, he also used plants even when he wasn't doing these stunts. Unlike some professed pickpockets who rely on shills because they can't do the act any other way, Rick's technical skills were excellent, and he often worked without preparing any of the volunteers. But Ricki had a well-reasoned attitude toward stooges: He felt that when a client books your act, he's paying for results. The client wants to see an audience roaring with laughter and gasping in amazement. How you get these results is your business. So Rick wouldn't hesitate to set up one or more of the fellows who would later be on stage with him if, for any one of a dozen reasons, he decided on that particular night, for that particular audience, it would guarantee the results the client was paying for.

It's interesting to compare Ricki with the other two most influential stage pickpockets, Borra (Borra was Europe's most celebrated pickpocket, and, sadly, he too past away just recently) and Dr. Giovanni. (Dominique, as well, could have been included in this group.) On stage, Borra was charming, compelling, regal and slightly imperious. Off stage he was a Mason, a gentleman farmer and a doyen of the Austrian magic community. He originally billed himself as "The Pickpocket of Kings and the King of Pickpockets." Dr. Giovanni was Giovanni every second. He would launch into his coin tricks and pickpocket pranks anywhere at all — at a restaurant, at the dentist and even in the barber shop! In front of an audience, his fractured English, irresistible charm and confident showmanship made him larger than life. He was accepted for membership into the prestigious Friar's Club, an organization for Hollywood luminaries. Both Borra and Giovanni spoke several languages; borders were no barrier in practicing their craft.

Ricki couldn't have been more different. He was, by comparison, a working man's pickpocket, someone who put on his uniform, went to work (Rick would say "Laid down a job") and came home. The thought of Rick, who was perpetually overweight and had a walk that approached a waddle, riding around a farm herding his sheep on horseback, as Borra did, or teeing off for 18 holes with the country club set like Giovanni, conjures up a most comical image ("Ludicrous" would have been Rick's word). He was shy about meeting spectators after a show, no matter how important they might be. His lack of education made him self-conscious, and he never wanted to be in a position where his absence of schooling or imperfect social graces might embarrass him.

On stage, he was a masterful combination of stand-up comic and steamroller. Off stage, he never tried to attract publicity, and he was not one to indulge in impromptu magic (though on rare occasions he would steal a watch from a fellow magician and later return it to the stunned owner). Rick was happiest sitting in a deli, surrounded by show business cronies, dining on split pea soup and rice pudding.

Actually, there were several different Ricks, and some of them were hard to be around. In a blink, a conversation could become a confrontation, and Rick didn't have a volume control to go with his booming voice. (Robert Orben suggested that Ricki was always eight seconds away from a full-bore screaming match.) An unintentional slight, seen through Rick's eyes, could become an unpardonable insult. Let's put it this way: you knew you were a close friend of Ricki's if he wasn't speaking to you.

He always let you know how he felt, and Rick felt everything deeply. He didn't wear his heart on his sleeve; he wore his heart on his sleeve in neon lights. Sometimes feelings clouded his judgment, and rash behavior affected his career. He walked out on more than one job for reasons compelling to no one else but Ricki.

For all of his bluster, if you were a friend, you *really* had a friend in Rick. Good mates were everything to Ricki who had little contact with his family after he left home as a teenager. Once he knew you as a friend, Rick could be a favor-doing juggernaut. He was also the softest touch in show business; appreciative recipients of his largess are countless. Rick would find a way to give money even when he didn't have it to give.

Part of the reason for his astonishing success was the single-minded determination with which he pursued jobs. He could be intensely persuasive with bookers. And he wasn't shy about applying this intensity on behalf of a friend. If he knew a performer who was right for a spot in a show (or was desperately in need of the work), a booker would experience the full force of Ricki's passionate lobbying. Many magicians owe plum dates to Ricki's faith in them.

Of all the name performers in magic, Rick was the most approachable. He had a wonderful ability to make the acquaintance of up-and-coming magicians wherever he went. There are hundreds of performers from Australia to London who consider Ricki Dunn the most important influence in their careers. He would watch their shows, listen to their grandiose dreams. Aspiring entertainers sensed in Rick someone who really noticed them, someone who took them seriously. With each one, he shared his show business moxie, sometimes improving an act dramatically with extraordinary suggestions. As I write this, I'm sure there are more magicians than I will ever know saying to themselves, "It was Ricki Dunn who gave me that line" (or that piece of business or that great idea).

Rick became friends with some of the most recognizable artists in our profession, performers like Norm Nielsen, Channing Pollock, Glenn Falkenstein and Glenn's wife, Frances Willard. He also shared his time with magicians who could most generously be described as journeymen (and less generously as hacks). Never condescending, not impressed by status, Ricki was exactly the same to everyone who held out a hand.

Ricki Quickies:

•"Have you a business card?" Of course you do, we all do. All of us? Ricki was a full-time professional entertainer for forty years, and he never once had a business card printed.

•His colorful, profanity-infused, speaking style came from years on carny lots and more years hanging around the wise guys who owned the niteries where he plied his trade. He didn't persuade; he "put the arm" on someone. He never traveled; he always "made a jump." If you could sing, you "had the box." He wouldn't negotiate with you, he'd try to "beat you down." When Ricki said "costume", he put the emphasis on the second syllable: cos-TUME. The way Rick pronounced the word "whore" rhymed with "lure" and came out "whoor."

•Did you know that Rick cut his own hair? In his early years, Ricki dated a wealthy young woman. One day she invited him home to the family mansion. The pair sat in the library awaiting her father. Dad walked in a few minutes later and said, "Excuse me, I was just giving myself a haircut." Rick was fascinated — this was a millionaire who could easily have afforded private barber visits. The fellow showed Rick how to do it, and from that moment on, Rick never saw the inside of a barber shop again. Quite a practical skill for someone who lived his life on the road.

•Rick married only once, and then just briefly. It was in the 1960s while he was performing in Las Vegas. He and his wife shared a mobile home. Physically, Rick looked more like a mob enforcer than a slick entertainer, so I was non-plussed when he casually told me one day that he enjoyed washing and setting his wife's hair. The image of this Mac truck of a guy daintily coifing his wife was quite endearing.

•He arrived early for every show; he felt it was the mark of a professional. He was fanatic about it. How early? One hour? Too risky. Two hours? Not safe enough. Ricki liked to get to the theater when the architect was drawing up the plans, just in case he had a few suggestions. Am I exaggerating? Not by much!

I can picture Rick doing any of the things he talked about doing — finding a new audience for his act in Laughlin, pitching slum behind a magic store counter, even operating a grab stand on the fair circuit — but I just can't picture him gone. The bible says we are allotted three score and ten years, but Ricki had to be early to everything. He died two months shy of his seventieth birthday.

Rick was never celebrated in the magical press, never recognized by those who bestow awards. Perhaps that's only fair since Rick *hated* magicians — or at least that's what he loved to tell me in expletive-laden fits. The obvious irony was that *he* was a magician, that all of his closest friends were magicians, that he would drive all day and all night to see a magic show, and that magic was the biggest part of every day he lived. But that's the same Ricki Dunn logic that allowed him to disparage every show he did while persuing bookings with the fervor of a zealot.

Ricki would be the last person to think of a legacy, but he did leave one, an important one. The peak of his career exactly filled the years between the great touring shows that ended with Blackstone and the magical explosion of the 70s. When magic was in its Dark Ages, he crafted an act built around his fiery personality and brashed his way into the big time. For those with eyes to see it, his act was a lesson in theatricality, combining so many elements — comedy, music, pacing, timing, internal structure, and novelty, along with real and perceived skill — into one commercially irresistable turn. Today when anyone — magician or laymen — tells me they once saw a pickpocket, the odds are better than even, the pickpocket they are about to describe is Ricki. His legacy is the four decades of people who will never forget the time they saw Ricki Dunn. His legacy is the hundreds of magicians he encouraged and inspired. And, most amazingly, for all his beefs and brawls, his legacy is a lesson in how to be a friend.

David Avadon ◈ 113

This article originally appeared in the July 1999 issue of *Genii* magazine and is reprinted with the permission of the publisher.

A Most Sympathetic Client: A Conversation with Borra

The first thing you must visualize when trying to picture Borra are his eyebrows: they're the size of shoe brushes. They dominate a face that's as round as the moon in a Méliès movie. If you are a film buff, conjure up an image of Oscar Homolka, add a dollop of Akim Tamiroff and you are close to seeing the Borra that strode toward me at the Beverly Hilton Hotel.

"Come, my dear, we talk," he said. (Men and women alike are "my dear" to Borra.)

For most magicians Borra was an unfamiliar name when it appeared in the trade magazines last year. (So unfamiliar it was misspelled several times!) He was to be honored with a fellowship by the Academy of Magical Arts, and I was delighted because I'd seen him on stage and greatly admired his pickpocketing tour-de-force. He more than deserved a Master's Fellowship for a

David Avadon ◈ 115

lifetime spent as a headliner in circuses and night clubs throughout Europe, for a lifetime spent emptying the pockets of unsuspecting volunteers whom he calls his "sympathetic clients."

We arranged to meet the day before he was to return to his home in Austria. As much as I had looked forward to spending time with him, it was mostly guilt I felt when we met. He should have been in bed. The twenty hour trek from their home in Graz, a small town in southeastern Austria, to Los Angeles had left Borra and his wife, Ilse, exhausted. After coming 6,000 miles, Ilse spent most of her visit getting a bed's eye view of her hotel room thanks to a virus acquired on the plane. Borra, too, felt awful, but he had struggled through his show at the banquet and wouldn't consider canceling our chat, or any of the other receptions and gatherings he felt obliged to attend. From the moment he emerged from the elevator he was BORRA.

It was the day of the Academy Awards (as in movies) and a crowd of autograph seekers had gathered at the hotel to snag the signatures of celebrities staying at the Hilton as they passed through the lobby to waiting limos. Among the star hunters was an amateur magician who had been at the awards banquet. He recognized Borra and spread the word that the man walking by was an internationally renowned pickpocket. The autograph hounds called out to Borra and waved him over. He posed for pictures and carefully wrote out greetings. It took me a moment to grasp the significance. Borra is

Serbian, Serbo-Croatian his native tongue. He lives in Austria where he speaks German. Though he can *speak* to audiences in many languages, at a moment's notice to *write* in English was quite an amazing feat.

Before we left, he turned to one of the women in the crowd and said, "My dear, Borra has a wonderful souvenir for you!" He reached into his bag and pulled out — her watch! We left to squeals of amazement.

And finally he began to tell me stories. (It takes concentration and a bit of psychic intuition to follow showman's yarns because, as one writer put it, "Borra ... uses the English language with the confident inaccuracy of a drunk at the controls of a jet bomber.")

Borra was born Borislav Milojkowic on April 26, 1921 in Jagodina, Serbia. His father owned a small clothing factory and had a marketplace stall where he sold the apparel he made. It was keeping watch over his father's stall that brought Borra his first encounters with shoplifters and pickpockets.

Something about picking pockets intrigued him from a very young age, and he experimented on school mates filching whatever he could. Soon he was returning pens and keys and diaries to his teachers, never revealing how these things came into his possession, simply saying he had found them lying about.

At fifteen he was already experienced at busking in the park, and he desperately wanted to join a circus. He ran away three times. The first two times his father sent the police to march him home. When he bolted for the third time, his father said, "All right, you can go, but you are not longer part of the family. I want nothing more to do with you."

Borra struggled for the next several years to find work, to invent the stunts that would bring the recognition he craved. Day by day, nuance by nuance, gesture by gesture, Borislav was transforming himself into BORRA. On the twelfth of January in 1939, he remembers the date exactly, Borra broke through in the most dramatic way imaginable. On that night he dazzled the king of Yugoslavia. When the king's chamberlain saw Borra's performance in a Belgrade night club, the dashing magician/pickpocket was invited to perform at the palace.

Borra beams as he remembers. "That night I stole de vatch from King Peter. After my show everyone at the party say to me, 'From now one you are BORRA — King of Pickpockets and Pickpocket of Kings!' "

Borra's father learned of his son's wonderful triumph at the palace, and welcomed him back into the family saying, "You've done more than make a success, you've become an artist."

And now there was a demand for Borra̲s and Borra met the need by performing a unique illusion — the multiplying pickpockets! Dragisa was his older brother and Vojislaw his younger. He taught them both the act, and dubbed them Borra II and Borra III respectively. Sadly, neither survived World War II.

By the time the Second World War reached Yugoslavia,

An elegant, early publicity photo of Borra.

Borra had developed a two hour show of magic, pickpocketing and illusions. Drafted into the Yugoslavian army, Borra staged grand entertainments for his fellow soldiers. On the pretext of gathering illusions for one last spectacular performance, Borra dared a dramatic escape from Yugoslavia. His odyssey brought him eventually to Vienna where he spent the remainder of the war years.

When peace arrived at last, he and his wife Ilse became naturalized citizens of Austria, and Borra moved his fast-

Borra hands back stolen articles to audience members he seemingly never touched.

fleecing specialty act into high gear. Wife Ilse had ties to the Kludsky family of Czechoslovakia, an important Eastern European circus dynasty, and the sawdust beckoned. Borra wanted to recreate his elaborate show which combined stage stealing with conjuring and self-invented illusions. He credits Ilse with talking him out of it. She counseled him to focus only on the pickpocket act. This, she reasoned, was the most commercial part of his performance, it was the act which brought him publicity and set him apart from other magicians, and, on the practical side, dropping the big stuff made it possible to travel with a minimum of impedimenta. Borra was wise enough to be guided by her insight.

In 1948, he scored an incredible publicity coup. Arnold Gingrich, editor of *Esquire* magazine (the editor responsible for bringing the top echelon of American writers to the magazine), was in Vienna probing for stories about post-war Europe. One night the expressive pen of Gingrich met the bravura talent of Borra, and the result was a three page article in the January 1948 issue of *Esquire* that reads like a Barnum broadside. (Though parts of the following stories may be apocryphal, all are the stuff of which great publicity is made.)

Gingrich first met Borra at a gathering of the American Army's Criminal Investigation Department (CID) which included General Mark Clark and Brigadier General Ralph Tate.

On Borra's appearance:

"The suave and courtly young Austrian who was introduced to the CID men ... may have appeared to some of them, in his trim elegance, as a type who might be better cast as ... [the] Commissioner in Charge of Viennese Waltzing."

On the group's response to his skills:

"The startled CID chief, no longer laughing, discovered

that his tie was gone from around his neck. ... at the very moment of his being introduced all around, [Borra] had managed, without attracting either the chief's attention or that of any of his men, to remove the former's tie .... Subsequently he had held their attention so closely with his talk about watches and wallets that nobody had looked at the chief to notice his missing tie until the moment chosen to point it out. The resultant uproar around American Army circles in Vienna was merely stupendous ...."

On Borra's antics at another military soirée:

"... he took the watches from the American, British, and French High Commissioners for Austria, and calmly 'discovered' them in the pocket of the Soviet High Commissioner. Everybody laughed — the Soviet Element loudest of all."

On Borra's early promotional ploys:

"... he worked the streets each day industriously striving to assure an increased attendance at his theatre each night. His method was to swipe the watches off as many of the citizenry as he could connect with in a day's conscientious endeavor, replacing each watch with a printed card to advise each victim, the next time he wanted to know what time it was, that Borra had taken his watch and that he could get it back that evening by claiming it on the stage during Borra's performance."

On the unique significance of his skills in post-war Vienna:

"His ... preferred victim for this culminating point in his performance is ... a Russian in uniform. For even now, over two years after the wild nightmare of the Red Army's orgy of 'liberation,' the sight of somebody taking a watch away from a Russian is the Viennese equivalent of seeing a man bite a dog. ... every time Borra [gets] one of them out onto the floor and begins looting him ..., you can sense ... that in the eyes of the breathlessly watching Viennese this ... debonair young man is acquiring heroic stature of ... mythical proportion."

On the demand for Borra's theatrical robbery:

"... Borra is practicing his bizarre blend of magicianship and thievery on a fine-art level in at least two Vienna night clubs every evening ...."

And:

"For ... weeks after his debut among the CID men Borra was kept busy swiping virtually everything but the pants off all the Allied High Brass around Vienna."

Just when one thinks Gingrich is going to scribble -30-,

he palms in a U-turn:

"Borra lives in an overcrowded, underserviced flat in a ramshackle and dilapidated area in the once beautiful Danube city .... The place where he lives [with a wife, a child] and a whole bevy of elderly female relatives, would be considered not only small, but of sub-slum rating, or rather condemnation, by American housing standards."

It's incredible, isn't it, to think of Borra doubling in two night clubs, in demand for every prestigious private party in town, then going home to a hovel?

Finally, Gingrich reaches his O'Henryesque conclusion:

"... when you see Borra in a night club, immaculate in evening clothes of flawless cut, his entire ... manner ... redolent of palaces ..., you would be ready to believe anything of him — even that he were Mephistopheles ... — rather than admit the inadmissible prosaic truth that he is a DP — just another of Europe's teeming thousands of stateless and homeless Displaced Persons."

What begins as a personality profile, ends as a revelation of the plight of thousands of people dispossessed and struggling for a livelihood in war-ravaged Europe.

Gingrich said Borra had an air of palaces about him. He should. He's entertained half a dozen kings and queens and carriages full of the lesser nobility.

"When I met King Frederick of Denmark, he greeted

me like a brother. We were both members of the same club."

When I asked about the club, the wily pickpocket became tightlipped, but then I guessed the Masons and he reluctantly admitted I'd hit upon it. Unlike the United States where locating a Masonic Hall is as easy as flipping open a phone book, in Europe, at that time, the Masons were a secret and quite prestigious order. Membership, as Borra discovered, could open even castle gates. (Interestingly, Dr. Giovanni, one of the earliest and most prominent stage pickpockets, was also a Mason, and quite proud of it.)

King Frederick's daughter married the future king of Greece, and Borra entertained this regal couple, as well as Juan Carlos of Spain, in 1963. Many years later, the queen sent a greeting to Borra via her son who was attending another royal shindig at which Borra was to be featured — in Los Angeles! Yes, dropping in to receive a fellowship wasn't his first trip to the City of smoggy-eyed Angels. In 1985, the charming highwayman was brought here to perform at a magnificent entertainment hosted by the Princesses Stephanie and Caroline to raise money for the Princess Grace Foundation. Borra was a great favorite of this royal family, having entertained them many times during his engagements in Monaco.

And what a bill to be on! The m.c. was Johnny Carson, the closing act was Liza Minnelli, and two of his on-stage victims were Charles Bronson and Gregory Peck.

According to Borra, it was in 1948 when he was

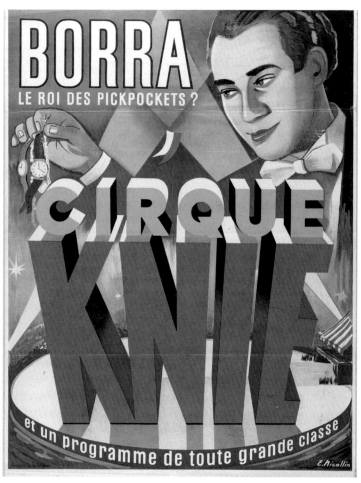

Borra brought the pickpocket act out of small cabarets and music halls into the center of the circus ring.

126 ◆ Cutting up Touches

appearing with Circus Knie, the national circus of Switzerland, that the manager of the show contacted Bertram Mills to suggest Borra would be perfect for his circus. Mills came to see Borra and was quite impressed, but an aide counseled that the act wouldn't go over with British audiences. The second time Mills saw Borra, this time in Sweden, he was convinced, and Borra was invited to join the Bertram Mills Circus, the most prestigious in all of Great Britain.

London had seen pickpockets before. Just after the turn of the century Fred Brezin trouped the British halls with a turn that included a spot of snatching, and he continued to play English theatres at least through the late 1920's. Giovanni, the Hungarian pickpocket with the Italian name, began performing in England in the mid 20's, and when he was "discovered" by British royalty, his career soared. He played the best English venues through the 1930's. By the 1940's Giovanni was bamboozling audiences in the United States, and the land of tea and crumpets was wide open for Borra.

And what an entrance he made into the arena! Borra entered astride an elephant, dressed as a character from the Arabian Nights, billed as the Thief of Bagdad. He began his act in a most startling way. He would say, "Would the woman in row 13, seat 7, please put on her glasses. You can't because Borra has them. Would the man in row 32, seat 10, please count the number of keys in his key case. You can't because Borra has it." He would open his turn by handing back items stolen from audience members seated sometimes hundreds of feet from the stage. How?

Years before, Borra had developed the ruse of dressing as a waiter or usher so he could indulge in some pre-show stealing prior to his performances. He would slide on a set of false front teeth to complete the disguise. (Borra slipped on the teeth for me. They are most comical.) So it was as a fumbling usher that Borra was able to steal the items that made possible an opening which non-pulsed the entire audience.

Like Houdini, Borra realized that it was the performer's responsibility to create such fascination with his skills that audiences *had* to come to the show to see it for themselves. So wherever the circus played, Borra, with reporter and photographer in tow, would visit the local constabulary, and under the guise of teaching the bobbies how to spot pickpockets, he would rob them blind to the huge delight of the local press. These hilarious publicity stunts assured packed houses and made Borra a top-earning circus star.

Though Borra rose to great stardom with the Bertram Mills Circus, his relationship with (Cyril) Bertram Mills once nearly collapsed. At the same time Borra was under contract to Mills, he was also being wooed by John Ringling North. North brought Borra to Havana where he was a tremendous hit. The circus magnate convinced and cajoled until he had Borra's autograph on a contract. The carrot Ringling held out was the chance to play Madison Square Garden. Borra contacted Mills and politely asked to be released from his contract. Bertram's reply was equally polite — he told Borra that if he didn't honor their contract he (Borra) would be subject to a fine equivalent to $8,000 and be barred from ever working in Great Britain again. So Borra picked himself out of the pocket of John Ringling North's contract and returned to England.

Borra has now been top of the bill for fifty years, wowing audiences on tours with European circuses — Krone, Knie, Scott, and Beneweis, to name a few — and in posh night spots like the Scala clubs in Barcelona and Madrid, Chez Paul in Brussels, and the Loews Hotel in Monte Carlo.

He has more than made up for the deprivations he suffered in World War II. Years of show business success have made Borra comfortably wealthy. He lives in a bucolic paradise on a farm in Graz on a roadway named for him — Borraweg — which honors his stature as an international celebrity. He is landlord to many properties in the area. His daughter Sesse, of whom Borra is intensely proud, is an attorney who makes a full time job of managing his estate. At one time Borra enjoyed breeding horses, but now sheep peacefully graze in the same fields where the thoroughbreds once romped.

Borra has been retired for some years now. Son Charlie is heir to his father's act and a circus star in his own right. Borra says of him with great pride, "He is *really* good!" But retirement doesn't mean to Borra what it would to any other performer. For Borra, retirement means that instead of touring *constantly*, he can only be lured away from his farm by pleading entertainment directors *most* of the time.

Several years ago I visited Madrid at the invitation of Norm Nielsen who was appearing in the review at the Scala - Melia Castilla — easily the equal of any showroom in Las Vegas. To my delight, closing the show was Borra. Night after night, I was able to see first hand how this indomitable showman created theatrical mayhem on stage.

When Borra saunters out in top hat, cape and tail coat he looks imperial, rather like a Russian general dressed-up in a magician's costume. His hat looks a trifle small on his very round head.

"I am Borrrrrra," he says, trilling the rrrs like a military tattoo. "Borra with two 'r's," he adds, fixing his name in the audience's mind from the very first moment.

The charm and joviality that define his on-stage persona are immediately apparent. He begins by producing cigarettes and blowing smoke rings as thick as fog. I've read many accounts of Borra's opening, all of them emphasize the smoke rings and what he does with them, but I was even more taken with how magical the cigarette productions seemed. He plucks a cigarette from invisibility, takes a drag, and discards it. He uses the smoke to form a perfect smoke ring, then, by inhaling, draws the entire ring into his ample nose — a most eerie effect. When it occurs to him to try something else, he finds another cigarette in mid-air to do it with. This time he blows a circle of smoke, draws out his pocket square, and passes it right through the center. Each cigarette production is so well motivated and so off-hand, the result is gasp provoking.

If a current of air disperses a smoke ring before he can nip his handkerchief through its center, he says, "Sabotage" in mock anger and does it again — and sometimes again and again until the stunt works to his personal satisfaction.

A bit of background before describing Borra's pickpocketing: Wish fulfillment is an important part of magic's appeal. We all wish we could cheat at cards, concoct the perfect bon mot, or whisk a rose into view exactly when it is needed. And we all wish we could tap a friend on the shoulder and hand back his watch and wallet to his thorough amazement. Pickpocketing is the ultimate in passive-aggressive behavior. And it's the reason audiences are enraptured by exhibition thievery.

There are three approaches to theatrical dipping. One is to create the illusion of pickpocketing through the use of stooges — spectators recruited before the show or discreetly asked to help during the performance. The next is to genuinely fool the on-stage helpers with adroit misdirection. (Dr. Giovanni and Vic Perry, when I saw them, were definitely in this group.) Put one and two together and you have the third approach: true skill mixed with a dash of collusion. Some pickpockets perform a magic trick which gives them a logical reason to handle the spectators. (Ricki Dunn's Bill in Lemon and Dominique's Bill in Cigarette are perfect examples of this.) Other pickpockets forego the magic and do their stealing using only verbal and physical misdirection. (Again, Dr. Giovanni and Vic Perry were examples of this approach. Although Giovanni used magic during his act, the tricks were separate interludes and not essential to the pickpocketing.)

Where does Borra fit in these groups and sub-groups? Simple: No stooges, no magic tricks — just pure misdirection.

After his last smoke ring evaporates, Borra takes a stroll through the audience greeting the guests at several tables.

"Buenas noches. ¿De dónde eres? De Barcelona! Bienvenidos! ¿Y ustedes? Suisa! Guten Abend, mein Heron. ¿Y estes señores? Inglaterra! Good evening. How arrre you?"

When he spots a likely candidate for his opening sequence, he invites the man onto the stage. As he asks him a series of questions, he spirits away the fellow's watch and several other items. Borra points out to the helper that he's missing his watch, which Borra promptly returns with a suggestion that the gentleman use his other hand to hold the watch tightly to be certain it doesn't leave his wrist again. Of course it *does* disappear again, and Borra leaves the audience with the strong psychological impression that the watch was stolen the second time while the man was still holding it!

Sometimes, while cruising through the audience

looking for likely assistants, he would just stop at a table, ask someone to stand, and do some stealing in the midst of the crowd. He has many little touches which play so strongly. He would rest a stolen wallet on the victim's shoulder while the person's attention was focused elsewhere, then turn to the crowd and say, "Look, he helps me!" If someone was touchy about being touched he would say, "Don't worry. Be happy." — a reference to the Bobby McFerrin song popular at the time. As an applause cue when sending someone back to their seat, he would gesture toward the man and say, "He's a most sympathetic client." (Sometimes he calls his audience recruits his "patients.")

Borra has two ways of doing the act. He can work single O or he can do a duet of dipping with wife Ilse. Ilse is blonde and statuesque, with a glamour that reflects several generations of stage savvy. Presumably Borra and Ilse simply decide before show time whether or not she will "suit-up." When she does, it adds an extra visual element to the routine. As Borra brings a man onto the stage, Ilse positions herself behind him. Borra then goes into his charming chatter, surreptitiously vacuuming the mark's pockets. In a ballet of thievery, everything he steals, he immediately hands off to Ilse, who, in a matter of seconds, is standing behind the fellow with an armload of his private possessions.

There are two signature stunts in Borra's repertoire of filching. One is the theft of a man's spectacles *while the person is wearing them*. And the other is his finale which begins with the nabbing of a necktie from one man and the suspenders from another, and builds from these thefts a situation which is hugely comic.

Borra doesn't work to a clock. Sometimes his ambles through the audience can last five minutes or more. While he's chatting up the customers, he is also mentally auditioning every guy in the club, looking for just the right person with just the right article to assure success with what's to come.

But even for someone as canny and perceptive as Borra, it's always possible for things to go wrong. Pickpocketing is the theatrical art form which most closely resembles bullfighting. Stealing techniques long perfected usually yield expected results, but human beings vary wildly in their willingness to be patted down and their willingness to play the part the performer has scripted for them. There's really no telling what will happen when an unsuspecting patron lured from his seat is bathed in stage lights and feels the eyes of the crowd upon him.

Borra's hidden reserves of showmanship are best revealed when things go awry. What happens if the person knows instantly that Borra has swiped his glasses? How can Borra deal with a spectator who jumps a mile whenever he's touched? Borra's finish requires that he steal a tie from one person and suspenders from another. But what if he doesn't spot a pair of suspenders (or a tie)? All of these things, and plenty of others, happened in the shows I saw. So what *do* you do when your ace in the hole flutters from your sleeve? If you're Borra, you just keep going, taking the disaster as a jumping off point for improvisation.

Here's one example of Borra's amazing recoveries: He's unable to find a pair of suspenders so his big finish is going to be stealing a necktie. As he is kidnapping the tie, he realizes that the fellow is on to him. Just think of it! This is the climax of your whole show and the mark has just tumbled! A pickpocket's worst nightmare! Borra is unflappable.

"You are worried about your tie? You think you might lose it? Don't worry. I tie it for you. I tie it extra tight to be sure you don't lose it. There you are. You have everything back now? Good! You may take your seat. You are a most sympathetic client!"

As he's knotting the tie, Borra steals it again and sends Mr. Observant back to his seat tieless — and clueless!

Because Borra has played mostly in Europe, it might be difficult for some to understand the magnitude of his success. So let's put Borra in American terms. (Naturally, his approach would have to have been adapted to suit American venues.) Picture a magician who becomes the starring attraction of the Ringling Brothers Circus and alternates his Ringling tours with seasons headlining the Cirque du Soleil. Think of a performer who divides his time between circus touring and long-running stints as the featured attraction in the revues at Bally's and the Tropicana. And who continues to be sought after at the most prestigious showplaces for *fifty years*!

Borra became a star when zoot suits were happening in L.A. His turn is so well structured and of such universal appeal that it still convulses audiences even in our current era of nose rings and pierced eyebrows. All of this with an act built entirely on skill with less props — a few cigarettes and billiard balls — than it would take to fill a child's lunch box.

As we finished our conversation, Borra extinguished his cigarette, took the last sip of his espresso, and said something extraordinary. He mentioned that he had just finished a season at the Tiger Palace, a night club in Frankfurt. And then he added, "They wanted me for next season, but I told them, 'No, it's too soon. I come back in three years.' " This chap is 76 years old. He came to prominence at the same time Judy Garland was dancing down the yellow brick road, and here he is nonchalantly booking himself into the next millennium! Borra is himself "a most sympathetic client." And for the hundredth time in an hour, listening to him made me smile.

This article originally appeared in the January 1997 issue of *MAGIC Magazine* and is reprinted with the permission of the publisher

Giovanni's Taking Ways

In this undated newspaper interview from the late 1930s,
Giovanni captivates writer Stuart Robertson

Not Even the Prime Minister's pants are safe when snatcher Giovanni prowls the premises, and the Scotland Yard Chief's wallet vanished as mysteriously as yours will if you don't watch out — but is all for a laugh.

The deftest pickpocket in the world has just informed me that he has no intention of reforming his taking ways, as he's a firm believer in the personal touch in his contacts with fellow humans. As he told me why, I listened to his alibi for a couple of hours, and it affected me so that I ended by agreeing that he should continue his nefarious career; I even promised to watch him do a little purse-lifting. And so I left him leering triumphantly in — not a cell — but a comfortable hotel room, for this was Giovanni, (that of course is not his real name) the dip who gives everything back.

David Avadon ◈ 137

Never mind his real name, which, due to his Hungarian origin, is more or less unpronounceable. Giovanni has done all right with his single adopted moniker, having become the pal of princes, the pet of London society and now he is over here fast becoming the delighter of American democracy. He is a stocky little man with wiry white hair, hypnotic black eyes, extravagant gestures, jumbled English, and a general aura of Continental mystery like a mastermind out of E. Phillips Oppenheim. And he's probably the only man in the world who … but let him tell it.

"My friend, the Duke of Westminster," said Giovanni, who tosses the names of the great about in the chummy manner of a man who is bumping into their owners at every bar, "often has me work his parties, and once he had me flown in a private plane from London to his country estate at Eaton Hall, where he was giving a binge for 500 guests. The huge house was open to them all, except for one dining room where the Duke had a dozen extra-special friends, and he took me aside before I went in. His instructions were to steal the braces off Winston Churchill at all costs, so I got the good sport who is now England's Prime Minister out on a chair in the middle of the floor. After lifting the usual articles off him I told him I was all through, but when he started to get up he found that his braces were gone. So he had to sit down to prevent an accident.

"He looked pretty touch for a moment, and then he said, 'You devil, I've heard of you before, and if I didn't like your cheek, I'd punch you in the nose! But I happen to like you, which is lucky for you, and so there'll be no hard feelings.' H e was laughing all the time, too, but nothing like the howls from the other guests. Believe me, there's no laugh to the aristocracy like seeing some celebrity afraid to take a step for fear his trousers will fall down."

"How can you steal a man's suspenders?" I asked skeptically. "If he's wearing a vest it will cover the top of his trousers, and he'd be sure to feel you fumbling."

"Stand up," invited Giovanni, and when I obeyed his hands slapped rapidly on the outside of all my pockets. "Wallet, handkerchief, keys," he enumerated, whirling me around and inviting me to sit down. Then I discovered that he had charitably loosened only the two front loops of my suspenders, and I had failed to feel the slightest touch on them. "That's how," said Giovanni, "and what's more, I could have pulled the whole works out from behind without your knowing it. Why? Because I never fumble.

"My proudest feat was done at a banquet given by Lord Trenchard, the head of Scotland Yard, for 200 of his junior officials. I was entertaining with my card tricks and patter, and I called the chief of detectives to help me. Right there before all those sharp-eyed fellows I stole his cigarette case, and not a one saw me do it. When I returned it he was flabbergasted, and then Lord Trenchard said it was lucky that I was an honest man, or the Yard would have a lot of grief over me. Later on I performed for the Big Five, which is the inner group of the highest Yard officials, but when I stole the braces off one of them he didn't see the joke. However, for the past six years I've been helping train the Yard personnel on how to spot pickpockets.

"Then," grinned Giovanni, I robbed King George IV when he was Duke of York. I snaffled his wristwatch during a dinner and as is my custom at the end of my act, I announced that I would distribute some souvenirs. I bowed to the Duke and offered him his watch. 'Oh, no, thank you,' said His Highness. 'You've given us a whopping good show, and that's enough. Thanks all the same. 'But you'd better take this one,' I urged, 'because it happens to be your own.' The Duke started to say that he had his on, then looked at his bare wrist, burst out laughing and led the applause.

"When the Duke of Windsor was the Prince of Wales he liked me to work at all his parties, and I've stayed in St. James's Palace a full 24 hours at various times. When I wasn't on the list of entertainers the Prince would call up and tell me to hurry over because the show was rotten, and off I'd dash. He'd be just as likely to take me along to entertain unemployed men at one of his Three Feathers Clubs as he was to have me at his fashionable parties. He was a good scout, I'd say. One splitting dawn we were both sitting on the pedestal of the fountain in Piccadilly Circus, and when a street sweeper said good morning to us, not knowing who the Prince was, the Prince told me to slip him ten shillings. I did it, too, and never swiped it back, and then we piled into a taxi and went off to the Palace to get a little sleep. Now, up to that time I'd never told the press about my activities with royalty but one day one of the papers ran a story with a headline stating we were very pally. I felt it necessary to explain to the Prince that it wasn't of my doing, and he laughed fit to kill. 'It's mine, Giovanni. I didn't think you were getting enough publicity, so I had arrangements made for the yarn.

"At the time of King George VI's coronation, I happened to be playing billiards in the Savoy Hotel when the Lord Mayor of London gave a banquet I thought I'd like to get in on it, so I bribed a waiter to change clothes with me, and then I went tin and entertained the diners with card tricks and fancy stealing. One of my tricks ends with my planting a card on someone, and that time I chose the Lord Mayer and told him the card was in his pocket. He was wearing all his glittering regalia and he searched all the pockets without finding the card. I finally had to show him where it was — in a small pocket far down the tail of his gold embroidered tail-coat. He told me he had worn that coat for four years without ever knowing there was such a pocket in it."

Giovanni has had experiences with certain gents who come to the stage with their pockets baited with fishhooks, broken glass and razor blades. He once caught a wise guy with a live rat in one pocket, but Giovanni forced him to turn it out before the audience and show what a spoilsport he was. The nonchalant chap with the butterfly fingers has suffered only one or two bad cuts, and now he's careful to gauge a pocket's contents from the outside before exploring.

"I had Leslie Howard with his trousers ready to drop off one night at Ciro's in London," confided the delusive dip, "and he sent me a photograph autographed 'To Giovanni, who nearly brought me to disaster.' I stole the watch off the late King of Siam at a private party given by Sir John Simon, and while there I also snaffled the watch of Aga Khan, supposedly the wealthiest man in the world. All he had in his pockets was a single shilling, and when he missed that he made more fuss about having me return it than he did about the watch. All through the entertainment he would pipe up to remind me that he was still short a shilling, so I prolonged his agony, to the delight of the other guests. When I gave the coin back to the Aga Khan he was so happy he told me to get a bet down on one of his horses that was racing the next day, but I forgot about it unit I happened to read that it came home first at 22-1."

Giovanni's high point in America was when he journeyed to Washington to entertain at the President's dinner for the Cabinet. There he stole the President's watch four times, lifted the suspenders of Brigadier General Edwin M. Watson, the chief executive's aide, and pinched all the cash from the pockets of that guardian of the Treasury, Secretary Henry Morgenthau. After his success Giovanni was asked to return in time for the White House correspondents' dinner, and this time he broke one of his rules. Sneaking the suspenders off the unsuspecting J. Edgar Hoover, Giovanni neglected to return them to the G-Man. They're now holding up the dapper dip's own pantaloons.

"When I applied to the American consul's office in London for a visa," said Giovanni, "I stole an official's watch for a gag, and he was then willing to describe me on my papers as a pickpocket. Well, when I reached New York an immigration man noticed the term, and nearly had a fit. 'You've got a nerve trying to come in here like this!' he shouted, and he called a policeman named Charley. I told Charley how it was, and he explained to the immigration man that I was an actor. 'Okay,' he said, 'then here are your papers.' 'Thanks,' I said, 'and here are your suspenders'.

"I leave the ladies strictly alone," said Giovanni, "as they have no pockets and are likely to keep their money in a stocking. Not that I couldn't get it even then, but I have a living to make and must think of the proprieties. Women are easy for crooked pickpockets, though, because they're so careless about their handbags. As a bit of advice I should warn them to carry their bags upside down and keep a firm hand over the clasp. No crook can open it then. And everyone should be wary of being bumped in crowds. If this happens, don't look where the bump came from — look the other way and you're apt to see something. And watch out for people carrying babies or bundles, as such burdens are a big help in letting a crook get close enough to you to work under cover of it."

"And how much do you make?" I asked.

"I got 150 guineas ($787) that time I flew north to joggle Winston Churchill's trousers, and my stage salary was 250 pounds ($1,250)."

"That looks as if crime sometimes pays."

"Not in this case," chuckled Giovanni, holding out a little roll of bills. "You'd better take this back, old boy. I happened to swipe it at the same time I was fumbling, as you call it, with your suspender buttons. You were a cinch, but there's a so-called hard guy loose in the world whose suspenders I'd love to loosen for good. His name is Adolph Schickelgruber, and I'd like to fix things so that the British will catch him with his pants — but I'm betting they'll do it anyway.

"So long, my friend, and watch your buttons."

So I backed out of the presences of the champion pickpocket congratulating myself that all my belongings were intact.

Or were they?

Excuse me while I take another look.

Index of Names

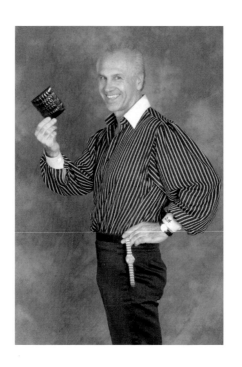

The Author

David Avadon travels the world as The Fastest Pickpocket in the West. He's been a featured entertainer for corporate events throughout the United States and in Singapore, Japan and Great Britain. He has appeared on national television more that a dozen times to demonstrate his light-fingered skills. On the ABC morning show, he managed to lift a spectator's watch, wallet and necktie in just ninety seconds. Celebrity pockets picked by Avadon include those of Michael Douglas, Pierce Brosnan and Tony Shalhoub. He has taught police officers and security guards the techniques for spotting dip artists on the street. He is a respected technical advisor, choreographing pickpocketing sequences for many films and television shows. The profile of Ricki Dunn reprinted in this book grew from their twenty-year friendship. For the opportunity to meet Borra and see him perform, Avadon traveled 6,000 miles, from Los Angeles to Madrid. The experience is chronicled in an article titled "A Conversation with Borra" which is reprinted here, as well. The idea for Cutting Up Touches was suggested by David Meyer, publisher of *Magicol*. The result is this, the first book ever written on the history and lore of theatrical pickpocketing.

www.davidavadon.com